follow you follow me

why social networking

is essential to ministry |

JOHN VOELZ

Abingdon Press
Nashville

FOLLOW YOU, FOLLOW ME
WHY SOCIAL NETWORKING IS ESSENTIAL TO MINISTRY

Copyright © 2012 by John Fred Frank Voelz III

All rights reserved.

This book is printed on acid-free paper.

Library of Congress Cataloging-in-Publication Data

Voelz, John.
Follow you, follow me : why social networking is essential to ministry / John Voelz.
    p.   cm.
  Includes bibliographical references and index.
  ISBN 978-1-4267-4196-8 (book - pbk. / trade pbk. : alk. paper)   1. Internet in church work.   2. Online social networksxReligious aspects—Christianity.   I. Title.
  BR99.74.V64 2012
  253.0285--dc23

                                                          2011045504

12 13 14 15 16 17 18 19 20 21—10 9 8 7 6 5 4 3 2 1

MANUFACTURED IN THE UNITED STATES OF AMERICA

CONTENTS

Contents

Post: Introduction

Getting Norma to try Twitter at first was an exercise in futility. She didn't want someone knowing what she did all the time and finding out things about her in order to drain her bank accounts and show up at her house uninvited.

I wasn't proud of my initial response to her. I thought I was going to shoot soda out my nose from laughing. I told her if anyone wanted to show up at her house uninvited there were a hundred thousand people in town and another hundred thousand on a NASCAR race weekend that just had to drive by. She didn't need a Twitter account to invite a home invader. The way I handled her opposition did not help Norma in any way and probably made her more paranoid. I apologized.

It didn't help that poor Norma often had her computer heisted by people (not me) in the office who played jokes on her, such as changing her desktop to a picture of George W. Bush eating a kitten or installing software that allowed them to control her keyboard from their smartphones.

Here's the thing: Norma is not a fuddy-duddy. She is the assistant of my copastor David McDonald. She has worked at Westwinds—the church where we pastor—for more than twenty years. She's actually pretty hip and is one of the most fun-loving and adventurous people I know. She has a smartphone. She uses Facebook. She can work a GPS. She uses a Mac and a ton of creative software. She's really funny. She likes to go to parties. She likes to try new things.

Some people will try to make the distrust or fear of Social Networking into an "old person's" ailment. Norma is twenty or more years older than I am. She didn't trust Twitter at first, but not because of her age. Just because you get the senior discount at your local pancake house does not make you shallow or boring or unwilling to try new things. Norma didn't trust it because she didn't understand it. She feared it because it wasn't explained to her properly.

One of our friends won't allow her daughter to have a Facebook account because of "stalkers and perverts." Her daughter is in her teens. She wants to have an account to connect with all her friends at church. Furthermore, the church uses Facebook to update the teens on what is happening next with events and missional activities. Her mom (our friend) insists it will only lead to trouble once her daughter posts pictures online and allows anyone with ulterior motives to take a close peek into her life.

Our friend is protective of her daughter. She loves her. And let's face it; stalkers and perverts are not a myth. They exist. Our friend doesn't understand how Facebook works, however. She doesn't understand that Facebook has privacy settings that can be enabled so that not just anyone can see her daughter's profile. Some of her fears could be put to rest if she would seek to understand.

These are real feelings. They can't just be pointed to and laughed at by forward-thinking, early adopters. The world is changing faster than parents can say *Sesame Street.* National media do not help with sensationalistic stories of cyber hate crime and virtual schoolyard bullies who influence suicide.

As such, we need someone to address the real questions, present real answers, tell real stories of redemption, and offer real hope to a world that has been caught in the quick current of changing communication.

"I don't have the time for that Facebook and Twitter nonsense." I've heard these words a hundred times over from people just like me, in similar work, life, and ministry situations. I've heard it from young and from old. From the "cool" and the "unlovely." Mac and PC. From geeks, techies, and the folk who are just starting to think that the Internet might be a big deal one day after all.

I've heard other critiques and responses: "It's a passing fad." "It's a pornographic cesspool." "I don't do that Twinkle-Twizzle thing." "I don't need to know about your gas problem or how late you woke up." "I don't want everyone knowing my business or when they can rob my house." And one of my favorite backhanded holier-than-thou responses, "I'd rather spend my time praying for those who use Facebook than actually using it."

I try to remind myself that these critiques and responses usually come from one of two places: fear or tradition.

In the long list of distractions that hold the church back from its mission, most fit cozily into these two categories. They aren't inherently evil, but they can thwart opportunity, make us bitter, distance us from our neighbors, breed cynicism, and turn us from a city on a hill into a curio shop in an alley.

Even people committed to ministry sometimes fear change and what they don't understand, are cynical of technological trends, have a hard time adapting to new customs and expectations of the world around them, and maybe don't understand why they even need to adapt to something new when they already feel taxed and exhausted and stretched.

There are real answers to fears from adapting to a changing world. The answer is not, "Shut up and deal with it." I wrote this book because I want to help you. I want to fill in the gaps. Answer the questions. Face the fears. And mobilize you for success in ministering through and enjoying Social Networking.

I've read many books that use a lexicon that resides in the lofty world of labels such as "postmodernity" and "post-Christianity." These books often talk about Social Networking, Social Media, and the Internet as part of the postmodern shift. Although these are helpful and I believe necessary, we cannot merely throw Social Networking into a postmodern pool. It has its own identity.

So, Why Me and Why Now?

I need to fess up. I was an early adopter. I was one of the first people I know of to sign up for Facebook or Twitter. Most rolled their eyes at me—except for the nerds, geeks, and other early adopters. I have always been a fan.

However, as an early adopter and eager experimenter I have tried, failed, and succeeded many times over with different applications of Social Networking. I've had a fair amount of traffic in the blog world with my blog at JohnVoelz.com, and I've had the privilege of working in a church environment that is very welcoming to new strategies and taking risks. Our church, Westwinds, has sparked the attention of *Time* magazine, Fox News, *A Current Affair, Newsweek,* the *Wall Street Journal,* and many Christian publications such as *Christianity Today, Relevant,* and *Collide.* In this process I have met many with opposing views, from apathetic to antagonistic, who are willing to converse about their stance on innovation, trends, culture, media, technology, and especially Social Networking.

As a pastor, I believe part of my role is to be an aggravator in the church at large—to get other pastors and church leaders to think about where we are and where we are (or should be) headed. In my conversations with pastors of all flavors, I've heard a high degree of apathy or disdain toward Social Networking.

I joined the world of Twitter in 2007 under two different names— one for my church and one for the leadership team that I am a part of. In January of 2008, I created the name "shameonyoko" as my Twitter username and began tweeting for myself—not just for the organizations that I am associated with. Since then, in no small part because of the attention our church received from hosting what is possibly the first ever "Twitter Church," where we used Twitter on multiple screens during the worship service, Twitter has been a part of my ministry life and conversation on a daily basis.

I'm a father and a grandfather—an extremely young-looking and vibrant grandfather who also believes in self-fulfilling prophecies. I've seen my oldest child experience the birth of the Internet and the appearance of the computer as a commonplace utility, source of entertainment, and communication device in our home.

My youngest two children have grown up with the Internet and Social Networking. They are as normal to them as growing up with television was for me. I've watched my granddaughter growing daily via the Internet and recently celebrated her birthday live via iChat and Facebook.

Until eight years ago, I never dreamed I'd have conversations about sexting, sharing dirty pictures and videos, trash talking, hate crimes, or virtual bullying. As a father and a pastor who counsels many families, I believe I have something to say to parents.

You don't have to be a teacher in the communication field to know students are communicating differently. The classroom battle cry "Stop passing notes" has become "I'm going to confiscate your smartphone." Many battles fought on the playground were birthed in cyberspace. Educators and influencers need tools to talk about this new language without children feeling shamed for using the technology we've given them.

It has only been a few short years since graduate-level students worked on a typewriter and met in the library. Now, notes are shared, concepts are discussed, and professors and classes are evaluated through Social Networking. Professors need to be part of and influence this new conversation. Social Networking is a great way to "get ideas into someone's head" rather than just "get the idea out of ours."

One of the best ways to understand new ideas or concepts, be they theological, technological, or cultural, is through metaphor. Throughout this book I offer a series of metaphors for understanding Social Networking. Some are familiar to church folk, such as the church lobby and the congregational prayer chain. I offer other metaphors too, such as the brief period in the hallway between classes at school and the provincial life captured in Disney's *Beauty and the Beast*. These images help us compare and contextualize this new space to worlds with which we are familiar.

Social Networking has scars. It has holes. It might not fulfill every task to the degree it advertises or like some people wish it would. But it's a "thing." It is not living and breathing, but it is a vehicle. Sometimes it's a tool. Sometimes it's a platform. Sometimes it's a care station. Sometimes it's an information source. Sometimes it's a connection point. Sometimes it's a bulletin board. But more than all these things, Social Networking is a new way of communicating, and it is not going away.

Post: Twitter Church and Cyberconfessionals

I found myself leading a struggling church the day I arrived at Westwinds. After a year of healing, mending wounds, and performing triage, we forged a team leadership model where three of us worked in tandem to lead a church committed to the idea of thinking differently. We rewrote the church values to reflect imagination, permission, authenticity, and community.

As such, we find ourselves trying things that have never been done in church. Many garner national attention. Positively inclined media quickly labeled us "early adopters," "gifted," "movers and shakers," and "mavericks." These labels are flattering but only partly true. We think what makes Westwinds special has more to do with freedom and willingness than with some special dose of gifting. There are people in your community who are looking for freedom to pursue God and willingness on the part of church leadership to venture beyond the norm.

Willing people. Willing leaders. When these two groups of people find each other and freedom and permission are granted, the church's potential is endless.

Twitter Sunday

A Westwinds idea that caught the media's attention was what we called "Twitter Sunday." Conceived in late 2007 and launched in 2008, Twitter Sunday (aka "Twitter Church") was an experiment in weekend church service participation that caught the attention of

Time, Fox News, CNN, and a myriad of other local and national media outlets.

The original Twitter Church experiment involved using multiple screens, increasing the bandwidth in our auditorium, inviting people to bring their laptops and smartphones, and providing classes on how to set up and use a Twitter account.

On Twitter Sunday, we encouraged conversation before, during, and after the service. We did not edit the conversation but let it happen in real time. We had five screens with ongoing and overlapping Twitter feeds. It was humorous, messy, insightful, challenging, emotional, worshipful, beautiful, and awkward. Such is the bride.

Posts ranged from silly comments on our attire and jokes about being late to church to deep questions about God and spirituality, prayer requests, struggles, and cries for help.

Since that original experiment we have used Twitter in various ways on the weekend, including having question-and-answer sessions, submitting prayer requests, posting words of affirmation and encouragement, exalting God, and conducting surveys in 140 characters or less.

Cyberconfessionals

Another Westwinds Social Networking worship gathering idea—perhaps my favorite—caught the attention of the *Wall Street Journal.* We called this idea "Cyberconfessionals."

We set up confession booths around the perimeter of the auditorium. Each confessional had a computer and a login screen for a Yahoo! chat group we had created. People were invited to log in as "Confessor 1," "Confessor 2," and so on, based on the number of their booth. The "confessees" who engaged them in conversation were made up of pastors, counselors, and ministry leaders from all around the globe. We recruited them to engage our people in conversation and hear their confessions. It was totally anonymous, although some people volunteered their real names.

All our confessees encouraged our confessors to make follow-up appointments with ministry leaders and counselors if they needed further help. Each of them was able to deliver the message "God forgives. He wants your surrender. He is willing to help. So are we."

The results were beautiful. The people we recruited to hear confessions reported that they were deeply moved and heard incredible stories. They were able to give good advice and offer help. Some confessors sought more help and made appointments with our staff, and one even checked himself into a suicide watch program. Social Networking allowed us to use a platform in a whole new way and incorporate an idea that has been around forever.

Using Social Networking in corporate worship has helped us:

1. **Meet new people.** Some people hid in the shadows for months (dare I say years?) and didn't feel as though they could participate in corporate worship until Twitter Church.

2. **Provide an opportunity for engagement and participation.** Some find the whole church experience foreign and don't know where to begin. However, engaging in cyber-conversation can be both engaging and a gateway for further participation.

3. **Spend more time with people outside of the weekend.** The classes we provide beforehand minimize fears about Social Networking, provide valuable skills, and give us an opportunity to meet with a group of folk to talk about the mission of the church and what we hope to accomplish.

4. **Get and give real-time feedback.** Social Networking screen feeds allow us to respond to questions and comments that

people are feeling in the moment. Even when comments are negative, we have an opportunity to respond in love, build bridges, speak the truth, and defuse bombs.

5. **Embrace changing technology and culture.** We have found that when we reference, talk about, and use technology in our services, we increase our chances of dispelling fears, educating, and demonstrating how Christians engage and enjoy technology and culture.

Not Everyone Thinks This Is a Great Idea

There are things we have done at Westwinds that would make many pastors raise an eyebrow or point a finger. That's fine. For the record, I don't care if another church uses Social Networking in corporate worship or not. I love it; I use it; but I don't have a Twitter mission. It has never been about a Social Networking agenda for Westwinds. It is about participation, new ways to connect with one another, reflection, interaction, and conversation. Regarding our church's use of Social Networking in church on the weekend, it is and has always been about creating a moment where we can all potentially respond to and move toward God in fresh ways.

The use of Twitter in corporate worship is highly contextual to a congregation. For Westwinds, the use of Twitter, among many other things, is appropriate for us but might not be for everyone. It is part of our culture of creative engagement with the gospel. It is expected that we will try different things. Some will fail. Some will become part of us.

I have a deep-rooted belief that God has called us to act upon the stuff in our heads. The thirst for the sacred, the mysteries of God, the magic of the sacraments, the otherworldliness of corporate worship, the tears spent on broken people—they call us to act. We act by creating—by making stuff. We can incarnate our thoughts into visual art, music, poetry, and film. Projects, proposals, and petitions. Moments and movements. And in this case, by using Social Networking in corporate church settings.

You need to ask questions and discover on your own which Social Networking application might work for you and your church. It may be time to try something new. It may be time to stir the pot. It may be time to go against all odds. And it may not be the time at all. However, you need to be on a path of discovery. The world is changing around you, and you need to exercise your imagination muscles.

There has been a fair amount of talk on the Web about the use of Social Networking in corporate worship settings, and it would be wise for us to examine what is being said. Below are some actual quotations and concerns we have received through e-mails, conversations, and posts on the Web, followed by some principles we can take away.

> There is a difference between communion with God and commenting on communion with God.

I can appreciate this comment as a worship leader who desires for everyone to be engaged in corporate worship at some level. However, this statement is only partly true. If the two were mutually exclusive, we would have to rule out the validity of antiphonal praise and chants and liturgical worship that calls for a leader to proclaim truths about God while the congregation repeats, responds, and gives the occasional "Amen." Sometimes, commenting on communion with God is very much a part of the communion.

If we're honest, there are many times we commune with or respond to God physically, and it takes our inside a while to catch up—if it does at all. For example, we might sing song lyrics to hymns and choruses that do not line up with how we are feeling at any particular moment. Nevertheless, we sing them out in hopes that our hearts will follow, and the words of worship become a self-fulfilling prophecy.

Takeaway: when we talk about God, he is listening and is part of the conversation.

> When in worship, worship.... Don't tweet while having sex. Don't tweet while praying with the dying. Don't tweet when your wife is telling you about the kids. There's a season for everything.

Although this comment comes from an honorable and great place of concern that we should be fully present and engaged in things that require our undivided attention, it's a bit of a straw man. The thing we need to be careful with is judging people for what we may deem distracting when it isn't to them. The very things that you may define as distracting to you may be things that actually help others focus, dig deeper, and engage.

In corporate worship environments, people need to be made aware of the rules. Social Networking in church is only out of line if it is understood that it has no place there. If you desire to create an environment where Social Networking is acceptable as part of the experience, you will have to educate your people so they know it is appropriate.

Scripture gives us much freedom in methodology and worship practices. But the makeup of your church might be a potpourri of traditions. Communicate expectations. (As an aside, sex is not purely physical. Most women will tell you sex begins in the morning. And if that is true, my wife and I are guilty of twittering during sex. We keep those twitters private, though.)

Takeaway: you must define the rules for corporate worship in your environment.

> Hearing preaching is heartfelt engagement in the exposition and exultation of the word of God. This is a fragile bond.... Perfume can break it.

> A ruffled collar can break it. A cough can break it. A whisper can break it. Clipping fingernails, chewing gum, a memory, a stomach growl, a sunbeam, and a hundred other things can break it. The power that flows through the wire of spiritual attention is strong, but the wire is weak.

The word of God is powerful. But to think that our ability to be affected by the word of God is so dependent on our ability to focus that the scent of perfume might derail us is frightening.

It is true that Twitter in church may be a distraction for some. But if it were true that the bond between what God is saying to me and my ability to focus on it is that fragile, we should get rid of the church bulletin, paint our walls white, put on peripheral blinders, and not move a muscle. (Then I'd fall asleep.)

Part of this comment may come from a place of concern that the Bible and its importance are diminishing in our churches. This may be a valid concern, but the Bible need not be threatened by other spiritual habits or creative worship.

Part of this comment may come from a place that values preaching as the apex of the weekend. I would suggest that whereas preaching has an important place, the apex of the weekend is more about meeting with God, however that happens. Through singing. Praying. Reading. Silence. Interactives. Social Networking. Video. A conversation in the lobby.

> Playing with my iPhone (or cell phone or Blackberry) during the sermon will likely distract me. I'll be tempted to check my e-mail or read my Twitter feed that has nothing to do with the sermon.

The first part of this concern cannot be controlled and is a matter of personal discipline. Being distracted by your smartphone in any environment is a matter of self-control.

The second part of this concern once again deals with the message being interrupted. To answer this concern, we first need to understand that it is a methodological problem, not a theological one.

Is preaching expository? thematic? systematic? Is it done in a series? with notes? without notes? for thirty minutes? forty-five? fifteen minutes, with a break for music in between? from the NIV? the King James? *The Message*? sitting? standing? on video? in person? with responsive readings?

The answer to all those things is…yes. And more. One would be hard-pressed to find a strict biblical model of an uninterrupted thirty-minute sermon preached while people sit in pews facing forward, hanging on every word.

Churches everywhere will interrupt their service this weekend with video, drama, and announcements. Once again, there is no prescription in the Scriptures for preaching a sermon.

If your methodology will allow for Social Networking to interrupt the message in order to enhance an argument or to call for engagement, then go for it!

Takeaway: to use or not to use Social Networking in church is a question of methodology, not theology.

Some of the arguments and concerns about Social Networking in worship services are the same arguments used for the past twenty years as churches have fought about PowerPoint and large-screen projection.

I remember one of our association pastors from California standing up one day and saying, "Men and women, there is a lot of talk about this PowerPoint. But the last time I checked, the power point was a man of God teaching the word of God to the people of God." It was followed by applause.

I didn't know what to do. I wasn't going to necessarily disagree; it just wasn't the point. Did using PowerPoint to project sermon notes and pictures somehow threaten preaching or the future of the church?

Is it possible to preach the word of God and to worship while inviting your whole congregation to comment and interact with you and others while you are preaching? Yes! Is it possible that is an act of worship for some? Yes! Is it possible that someone will engage and be engaged better by use of this technology? Yes! Is it possible that communion with God and commenting on communion with God are not mutually exclusive at all times and that perhaps one can affect the other? Yes!

Is it for everyone? No. Is it possible it will distract? Yes.

So will bad preaching.

Is it possible to worship God without a thirty-minute sermon at all on a Sunday? We had better say yes or we have got a lot of conversation ahead of us.

Instead of talking about ideas of what is proper and what is not for church, let's talk about what is working and what is not. Let's share stories. Let's celebrate what God is using. We have only begun to discover what Social Networking is capable of, and we are in many ways in the experimental stages of this technology.

More Ways to Use Social Networking in Church

Using Social Networking in your corporate worship service may or may not be your thing. It might not match your church personality. That's fine. Here are some other ways you might consider taking advantage of Social Networking before, during, and after what happens on the weekend. We have tried all of these to various degrees and with various results.

Have breakout discussions during the service.
Reserve ten minutes or so for Twitter banter about a topic, the message, a passage of scripture, and so on. Have the band play some instrumental tunes, or put on an appropriate soundtrack for the mood.

Put twenty Twitter plants in your audience and tell them the things you want them to reiterate on the screen at the end of the service.
One Sunday we did this with a group of people who were not already involved in other areas of ministry. I told them that they were the "new worship leaders." Because worship is a response to God and it is participatory, these men and women were given an opportunity to influence the feel of the weekend and to invite people to respond. Even those who were not actively twittering along with the group found it helpful to hear the insights of others.

Give permission for Twitter at any time—even when it is not on the screens.
Get your people sharing their thoughts with one another. It is comforting to hear that others are thinking the same things or asking the same questions as you.

Communicate with your tech booth, ushers, nursery, or whomever through Twitter.
Last week I twittered that it was hot in the room. The ushers got right on it. But more than just communicating what needs to be done, it is helpful to have an ongoing conversation with those who are serving with you, in order to get feedback, make changes, adapt, and celebrate together. Sundays always feel better for me when I grab five minutes to read the Twitter roll about how people are responding and enjoying corporate worship.

Have your other staff Twitter with the message and guide the conversation to what you want people to remember most—sometimes the staff members who don't have an active role on Sundays want to feel like they are part of making it special. Invite your office staff and administrators to guide a conversation, making note of special points you want people to take home with them.

Twitter questions and answers.
We have had great success with reading questions from a feed on the screens and responding in the moment.

Create end-of-service onscreen surveys.
The sky is the limit. Ask questions about the songs you are doing, the series you are in, the summer children's program, the lobby hospitality, or anything you like. Get real-time feedback.

Text your vote.
Put up a list of songs at the end of the service and ask people to Twitter which ones they like and don't like. Ask people to vote on the next message series.

During the service send messages to missionaries and those in cyberland.
In 2010, I sat in a room of creatives in Franklin, Tennessee, at the re:create conference. Mark Jaffrey, a friend and pastor in Egypt, was there during the uprising that was taking place to overthrow the government. We had a video feed of Mark on the screens. Twitter messages came at Mark at lightning speed while we asked questions about his safety and what God was doing in the midst of the chaos. I cried like a baby while hearing from Mark. The tweets that followed the live video portion continued for weeks as Mark filled us in.

Promote events on the screen that are happening throughout the week.

Encourage the congregation to interact with your elders and other church leaders.
Let people know that your staff and elders are all live on Twitter and that they want to interact.

Line up fifty people to give 140-character testimony or faith stories during Communion.
Stories are powerful. Have people Twitter instances that they remember that tell how God has pulled them through or shown his faithfulness.

Script an entire Twitter conversation and gather fifty people to help pull it off.
Just as a drama would unfold before everyone's eyes, communicate a powerful story or situation through the use of Social Networking as if the story were unfolding in real time.

Do a Twitter scripture reading.
Split up your scripture among as many people as you like and have them Twitter the scripture in sequence on the screens.

Do a ministry fair blitz through Twitter.
Between or after church services, get all your ministry heads present on Twitter talking about how to get involved with their area of ministry.

Schedule a postservice Twitter application group focused on the message for the day or the current series you might be in.
Some of our satellite groups (small groups) around Westwinds have formed organically through groups that regularly communicate through Social Networking. They met online and then met up face-to-face.

Have your people Twitter links to their favorite inspiring websites.

Ask people to Twitter their burning questions about the service.

Promote the ministries of the church in 140 characters or less.
For example: @shameonyoko is waiting at the coffee bar to talk to you about the band. @loritate is dying to tell you about Kid's Journey after Fusion. Come down the hall for snacks. Join @shameonyoko for a beer at Westpoint tonight at 6:00.

Have your people send out their prayers of encouragement to someone who can't be there.

For example: @shameonyoko says, "I am praying for your peace." @normzie says, "We are so proud of you guys working in Mexico. We are praying for your strength!"

Start a Facebook group and invite the congregation to join the conversation.

Creating a Facebook group is an easy way to find like-minded people or people who are interested in talking about specific topics. It's always good to know your audience. Sometimes it's a guessing game in a public forum, but Social Networking groups help leaders be sure that the people who are involved actually want to participate.

Create a hashtag (#theylooklikethis) on Twitter and tell your followers to join the conversation.

Hashtags are a way to aggregate things topically on the Web. If I create a hashtag called #jesushateshockey, then everyone who uses that hashtag in their tweet will have their comments aggregated in one spot on the Web for an easy way to follow the conversation while I make fun of my Canadian friend who just watched his Canucks lose their stab at the Stanley Cup. You can make your hashtags more meaningful if you like.

Create a hashtag for your church so the congregation can follow conversations with the leadership.

At times, we create hashtags to give people insight into a conversation we are having internally—perhaps during a conference we are attending, or perhaps when we are discussing a topic of debate. Hashtags help people who aren't able to be involved physically to feel like they are part of the action. When I go to concerts and conferences I often use hashtags to keep people up to date on my experience. This gives us food for fodder at later times and makes people feel like they are experiencing it with me.

Post updates about needs in the congregation and situations people can potentially respond to directly.

One couple needed thirteen thousand dollars for an adoption. After reading their blog post, which they had linked on Twitter, someone wrote them a check. A mom told her husband on Facebook that the air conditioning went out, only to have a serviceman show up at the door and fix it free of charge thirty minutes later. A couple's house burned down, and the congregation responded with gift cards to feed them and pay for their gas while they rebuilt. All these needs were met in a timely manner through Social Networking.

Share prayer requests and updates.

My friend Randy died of cancer a few years ago. His online posts throughout his struggle and the posts of others regarding his health were a source of strength to all of us. I have other friends currently struggling with health issues. Social Networking continues to be a way to encourage families in need and for them to give updates to a large group of concerned people all at once.

Uh-oh, How Do I Respond to This?

Because I am such a fan of using Social Networking with your church, and we have tried so many experiments, I thought it wise to end this chapter with a fair warning from our experience—or more specifically, from my experience.

One of the criticisms ministry people have with Social Networking is that it can be addictive. It is always there, it is hard to get away from, and it can be exhausting.

I'm not going to lie. All this is potentially true.

I say "potentially true" because it has happened to me—and to my friends. But it doesn't have to be this way. We have also learned ways to protect ourselves and to make sure we are in control of the technology and not the other way around.

I was not good at this early on in my Social Networking escapades. My Twitter account and my Facebook account were set up to send me e-mails and text messages on my iPhone at all hours of the day. It was superfun at first. I heard from a ton of people I hadn't talked to in a while and met many new people from church. It was exhilarating. Then it got tough.

All of a sudden, I was always available. *Always.* And with messages and updates coming to me at all hours, I found myself asking questions in a way that I had never had to ask before. "Do I really care about this need?" "Do I know this person well enough to muster up sympathy?" "Is it my role to respond to this or to someone else's?" "How important is this thing that this person is making out to be an emergency?" "Do I send a message now or wait until morning?" "If I open this door, am I inviting this person to contact me at home like this all the time?"

At the church office if someone has a financial need we put the person through a process. There's an application, an interview, and a series of questions the individual must answer in order for us to best help her or him. There are certain days on which we look at these applications. There are people dedicated to it. These processes and boundaries are the same with many things at the church office: counseling, crisis management, staff meetings, which days reimbursements are made, days off, and what we can and can't do on a Sunday, for instance.

In the early days of Social Networking, everyone's role, the processes, and the boundaries all got mixed up. It was no one's fault. It was a learning process. Those who joined Social Networking platforms saw me as available to answer anything and free to meet any need at any time of the day. And they took advantage of it.

What do you do with the mom who sends you a Twitter message saying her baby has no food and Dad just walked out? What about the guy who is contemplating suicide and Facebook alerts you in the middle of the night? What about the person who just realized his need for Jesus and wants to talk to you about baptism at 9:00 p.m., when you just sat down with your spouse after a hard day?

Let's first realize that this is not a problem of the technology. The technology presents new questions that we have to answer for ourselves about time management and responsibility, for sure. But the issues of time management and responsibility stand on their own in multiple venues and stations of life.

There are boundaries and safeguards you can set up in Social Networking platforms, and preferences you can set in smartphone apps, to help minimize potential unhealthy fallout. And you need to know it doesn't have to be all-consuming. You have choices. You have routines. You have commitments. It's important to learn to manage Social Networking so that it doesn't manage you.

Here are some things to consider:

You may want to set up a time when you plan on checking your Social Networking platforms and limit yourself to that time. I do this in many areas of ministry. I only counsel on Wednesdays. I only allow myself to run one satellite group at a time. I don't answer my phone after 5:00 p.m. I don't talk church business with staff once I am home. Some limit their Social Networking to certain days or to only so many minutes a day.

If you have an addictive personality, take drastic measures to set boundaries. If you have decided to get started with Social Networking and you are easily distracted and addicted, or if you are currently swimming in a Social Networking whirlpool that sucks all your time, you might need some disciplinary tactics:

- Leave your computer at the office at night.

- Turn off your smartphone.

- Set your preferences in Twitter to only notify you during certain hours.

- Don't allow your tweets to go to your SMS on your phone like all your other text messages.

- Don't allow Social Networking to alert you through e-mails when you receive new messages.

You may want to create proprietary spaces. These are the spaces dedicated to engaging in certain activities and only those activities. When I was growing up, I could not bring my toys into Grandpa's den. That was the spot where he unwound, smoked a pipe, and watched TV. It was dedicated. Pick an area (a desk in the lobby, a coffee shop, and so on) as the place where you engage in Social Networking. Sometimes when we limit ourselves to spaces, it enables us to create other sacred spaces that become an important part of our ability to disconnect, meditate, rest, breathe easy, remove distractions, study, pray, and so forth. If you sit at your office desk and have a hard time knowing whether to do the schedule, make the call, read the book, do the follow-up, or check your Facebook, you may need to create proprietary spaces.

Communicate with your church and let them know your boundaries. Get good at telling people you only answer your phone until 5:00 p.m. Post messages on your Facebook status letting people know that you are having quality family time. Tell people you don't do Social Networking while on vacation. Whatever your particular boundaries are, communicate them and stick to them.

It isn't always urgent, and it isn't always your emergency. Don't get caught in the trap of thinking you have to answer everyone's theological query. Don't believe for a second that God wants you to answer every need or drop what you are doing to respond to everyone.

The nature of Social Networking is such that at any given time there is something that begs for someone to address it. That doesn't mean it's you.

Set your Facebook chat status to "offline." At the bottom of your Facebook page, there is a chat box that allows people to see when you are online. This means they can interrupt you at any time. It may not be a pressing need. Most of the time it isn't.

Sometimes Social Networking is like going to a missions conference where presenters talk about the particular horrific situations and needs of their country and how you can help. I sometimes leave those conferences feeling like, if I am going to be a good Christian, I have to buy all my fair-trade coffee from this vendor, buy my shoes from that vendor, support this child in Uganda, buy this freshwater drinking straw, and purchase this whole video series that funnels profits into an organization to combat the sex trade.

But if I left those conferences responding to every need, I would soon be out of a job for lack of time and focus; I would lose my home from spending too much money; and I would eventually lose my family because I was a bleeding heart who couldn't take care of needs at home while I tried to save the world.

Yes, we have a responsibility to one other. This is why we got into ministry in the first place—to love the unlovely; to spread hope; to tell people there is good news; to make room for the stranger. Managing our involvement in Social Networking does not negate these things.

When we set up Social Networking safeguards and boundaries, we aren't ignoring people or abandoning them. We aren't saying they don't matter. We are being proactive and smart so that we have the energy to focus on the specific things God has called us to do with the time, energy, and resources that we do have.

Conclusion

Regardless of whether you use Social Networking in corporate worship, during the week, only on weekends, or on your smartphone; relegate it to your media room at the church; or don't use it at all, it doesn't really matter. What matters is that you are asking the questions about what works for your specific ministry scenario, lifestyle, and personality.

The fact remains that whether you are using Social Networking or not does not change the reality that it is here to stay and it is morphing into new forms and platforms every day. And your congregation is using it.

I heard a joke when I was in Romania a few years back:

Q: "What do you call someone who speaks three languages?"
A: "Multilingual."
Q: "What do you call someone who speaks two languages?"
A: "Bilingual."
Q: "What do you call someone who speaks one language?"
A: "American."

Europeans think this is hilarious. I think it's embarrassing—maybe because I was told the joke in English by a Romanian in the company of a German and an Italian who all laughed at me. I was their example in the mush pot.

There are many reasons that Europeans are multilingual. For instance, there needs to be a default language for worldwide business in an ever-shrinking global economy. Also, European countries have close borders like U.S. states—languages don't up and stop at a border, so people on the fringes of those countries have learned the languages and dialects of those neighbors surrounding them. However, the fact remains for many of my European friends that learning

31

other languages was a priority for them, unlike me who took a year of Spanish, got bored and skipped to French, and then quit studying both with only enough retention to recall the cuss words and how to ask where the bathroom is.

I have missionary friends in Europe who have mastered multiple languages in order to be effective in an economy where they are breathing the gospel into a diverse makeup of people. See where we're going?

Social Networking is not a fad. It is a new way of communicating. Whether your church is a forward-thinking midwestern church, you live on one of the coasts, or you belong to a small passive congregation, this new way of communicating is affecting you, your children, your grandchildren, your neighbors, your real estate agent, and everyone you are called to love for the sake of the Kingdom. They are speaking a new language. It is a default language. You may not become fluent in every situation overnight. But you need to learn it.

During the writing of this book, I asked my networks to send me notes, posts, messages, or e-mails regarding their thoughts on Social Networking and ministry. I appreciated the following response, which spelled out our responsibility to one another (not necessarily *for* one another) as Jesus followers in a Social Networking world. This reminder points out that Social Networking is not always so much about what we are communicating to our churches, but rather what the world is communicating to us. Karysa wrote:

> A status update is the modern message in a bottle, the new soapbox to stand on, a way to air dirty laundry and wear your heart on your sleeve.

> People will post things that they'd never just bring up in conversation. Is it sad? Maybe. But, it's true. I often read through my Facebook news feed and just pray for people. I can ask God to help them with specific things in their lives that I would have had no clue about, had they not updated their status.

I pray for their job interviews, their sick kids, and their bad days. I can easily post a comment of encouragement or refer them to a helpful Bible verse.

Some people find social networking impersonal or a poor substitute for in-person connection. But, I think that without it, we would be missing huge opportunities to share God's love with people.

Times are changing. If we as Christians don't adapt, we will lose more than opportunities to make "friends"; we will lose opportunities to make brothers and sisters in Christ.

Well said.

Learn the world of Twitter with the supplemental guide *Tweet You Tweet Me: A Startup Guide for Churches,* available through Abingdon Press and ebook retailers. Go to www.abingdonpress .com/Voelz for more information.

Post: The Wrong Questions

The School Passing Period

Out of all the objections I hear regarding Social Networking, the demonization of its inability to properly interpret tone and other nonverbal communication is probably the one I hear most.

I understand this objection. I taught communication labs at the college level, and one of the first things students learned in them was, "People will believe your nonverbal communication over your verbal." The *way* you say things is paramount to *what* you say. You can say the words "I'm sorry" to people ten different ways and mean ten different things. You can be sarcastic, dismissing, angry, or genuine. Social Networking leaves all that up for grabs. People are left to interpret your tone based on text and what they think they know about you.

This is why Social Networking should never be used as a vehicle for conflict resolution. Like e-mail, it is easy to write something we will one day regret and hit the send button without thinking it through.

But we can't throw out the Social Networking baby with the bad communication bathwater. The baby is innocent. There are rules and etiquette for communication with any technology and situation. It isn't fair to spank the baby for something she didn't do.

When I was in middle school and high school, my favorite times of the day were in between classes. We had ten minutes to move from one class to the next. In that time, we gossiped, talked music and movies and fashion, complained, celebrated, caught up, sneaked a quick kiss from a girlfriend or boyfriend, grabbed a snack, and quizzed one another for the upcoming test.

Sometimes, however, the passing period was just enough time to get in trouble, antagonize, aggravate, pass breakup notes, or flip off the kid who couldn't get to us fast enough to punch us.

The passing period is full of good and bad potential. We need rules and we need tools to navigate the hallways.

Brunilda used to be part of my church. She was always getting herself in trouble in the Social Networking world. She would call people out on Facebook, post "prayers" that mentioned people by name as well as their particular sins, wax political, and guilt-trip people into having the same opinion as she did, which, in her mind, was Jesus' opinion too. She headed full speed into Social Networking, not caring about the fallout of her reckless opinions, causing hit-and-run accidents as she T-boned other passersby and fled the scene of the crime.

People tired of Brunilda really fast. I had many talks with her: "Please don't post these things." But she didn't listen. She lost friends in a hurry. No one wants to be berated with messages from naysayers and zealots. It was depressing.

Brunilda reminds me of the girl you might pass in the halls between classes who doesn't have the guts to say something to you in a venue where you can talk it through and work things out. Instead, she chooses to walk by you and make rude comments or throw a slushie in your face before class starts, and you have no way to defend yourself or even ask what you did to get her so riled up.

Many people "unfriended" Brunilda. I wanted to many times. However, as her pastor, I kept an eye on her. I chose to live by that "keep your friends close and keep your enemies closer" rule with her. One thing is true of Social Networking: good, bad, right, or wrong, someone, somewhere, is probably saying something about you or your church online. Social Networking sometimes gives us a window into the opinions of our people that we might not otherwise have.

Brunilda still breaks the rules from time to time. However, her online rants have also given me an opportunity to pull her aside and chat about some important things. She has asked for forgiveness on more than one occasion. Sometimes she is exhausting. But if it weren't Social Networking, Brunilda would make her presence known in other venues. And she has, for a long time.

Matt, conversely, is one of my favorite people to pass in the virtual hallway. He knows time is short so he uses his words and his time wisely. He is always telling the rest of us about concerts coming up, new bands, and great news. He is quick with a joke. He's the guy you look for in between classes. You want to be around him.

In middle school and high school, I distinctly remember passing people who were crying. Sometimes people had their arm around them comforting them. Other times they were alone. Being a bleeding heart, I always wondered if I could help somehow. Occasionally, I would comfort the nerd who had just gotten slammed into his locker by the bully. I remember a quick chat with one girl that led to me to praying with her after school about a situation at home.

The school passing period often gives us enough information to go on, as we are on our way to something else, to allow us to continue the conversation, perhaps during the next passing period or perhaps after school.

In his book *Here I Am: Now What on Earth Should I Be Doing?* author and speaker Quentin Schultze points out that believers in Jesus have choices to make about how they will respond to any given situation based on both their vocation (the shared role of all Jesus followers to be caregivers to one another) and their individual stations (their particular jobs, situations, and roles as parent, sibling, coworker, boss, pastor, musician, artist, and so on). In both vocation and stations, Schultze says nurturing friendships and community is a godly mandate. Nurturing friendships happens while engaged in relational activities and while listening to one another's respective life stories.

Schultze points out that godly love in action looks like friendship, hospitality, and neighborliness. "Making room" for the stranger among us is Jesus' example. Social Networking is a vehicle for just that. We meet strangers in the passing period. We hear bits and pieces about their lives. They follow us; we follow them. As followers of Jesus, we have an incredible opportunity to be listening ears with potential friends in the hallways during the passing period.

Three Categories & Three Questions

In early 2011, the news website Mashable reported that Charlie Sheen had set a Guinness World Record. Actually, he had invented a whole new category of world records. On March 1, while experiencing the heat of one of his many controversies, he joined Twitter. Within minutes Sheen had more than sixty thousand followers—before he even tweeted. In just over twenty-five hours he had more than a million followers, giving him the record for "fastest time to reach one million followers."

Simultaneously, Sheen's escapades with drugs and strippers, and claims of having "tiger blood," got airtime. His annoying phrase "Duh, winning" was repeated by every comedian on television.

Unfortunately, Social Networking news stories like Charlie Sheen's strengthen negative opinions and impressions of Social Networking's usefulness and redeemability. The most common arguments and questions surrounding Social Networking and its viability and usefulness to the church can be fit into three categories:

1. The Church's Role and Responsibility in the World
2. The Christian's Role and Responsibility as the Church
3. The Church's Role and Responsibility to the Church

Consider a few examples.

1. The Church's Role and Responsibility in the World

- "Technology is not helping us connect with the world. It is distancing and *distracting* us from one another."
- "Why do we always get distracted by the things the world values?"
- "With all the bad things that have happened through Social Networking, such as bullying and pornography, isn't it better to distance myself and my family from its lure?"
- "Do we always have to be the church of what's happening now?"

2. The Christian's Role and Responsibility as the Church

- "Where am I going to find the *time* to do this?"
- "I wish people would devote the same amount of energy to serving our city that they do updating their Facebook status."
- "Would Jesus be sitting at his desk or glued to his iPhone?"
- "Ministry is hands-on!"

3. The Church's Role and Responsibility to the Church

- "Is this real *community*?"
- "We have become increasingly isolated as a people and need to educate others on the importance of face-to-face interaction."

- "If we use Social Networking in the worship service or through the week, aren't we distracting from the message and the real reason we are all here?"

These are all categories and questions of mission—"Who am I and what am I supposed to be doing?" They aren't bad questions. We should be asking ourselves questions about our individual role and the Kingdom role we play. But the questions aren't always valid at face value. Sometimes there are questions behind our questions that should be asked first.

For instance, if I ask, "Does your church have good music?" because I am thinking about attending there, you can derive from that question a few things about my personal bent and what I understand to be valid about church. First, I like music. Second, I like a particular kind of music that I categorize as good. This means I also have ideas about what is bad music. I also believe that music should be a part of church. Not only that, I probably think music is one of the most important things that happens there.

If someone asks you a question like this, it is good to have a series of questions to follow up with. If we go beyond the initial questions, we begin to stir up presuppositions and postures that those questions are based on. Sometimes there is a better question or series of questions that get to the root of concerns.

The questions and categories crossbreed with one another. They aren't tight categories. The categories represent the roadblocks that arise in the arenas we do life in as Christians.

Three of the most popular words that get tossed around in the debate of role and responsibility (as seen above) are *community, time,* and *distraction.* They come up time and time again in various contexts, so let's zero in on them.

What Is Behind the Community Question?

Let's start by examining a question: "Is Social Networking real community?" This is a key question for our role and responsibility in all categories (though it most often comes up in conversation about how the congregation should respond toward one another as a community of believers). Concerns, fears, and misunderstandings about community, the lack of it, and the validity of its existence in Social Networking may be the number one deterrent for Social Networking being utilized for the sake of the Kingdom.

When I get asked this question, I assume a few things that may or may not be lurking behind it:

- Community is important to the individuals who ask this.
- They have a specific idea of what it is and what it is not.
- They probably believe community is something that everyone needs.
- They don't want to make bad decisions regarding community nor do they want others to make bad decisions.
- They might be suspicious or fearful about something that seems like it offers a false promise.
- They probably have experiences that shape their idea of "good" community.
- They might think there is an ongoing problem in the church regarding community.
- They probably have a fear that we, the human race, are losing or masking the value of human touch, which, if true, presents some real dangers.

A *Siren Magazine* online article entitled "If God Had a Twitter" (www.sirenmag.com/?p=316) reflected many of these fears by mocking claims that Social Networking is "community" at all.

The article references the book of Hebrews: "Don't stop meeting together with other believers, which some people have gotten into the habit of doing. Instead, encourage each other, especially as you see the day drawing near" (Hebrews 10:25); compares Social Networking with face-to-face communication; and decides Social Networking is inferior. The argument is presented that "communication through technology" is disembodied and more prone to misunderstanding, especially in worship. It even includes this zinger: "It's hard to teach people about the glories of the incarnation while disincarnating yourself online."

The article voices both a concern that there is a lack of community in the church and a strong skepticism that Social Networking can somehow help fix it. It echoes a popular belief that when the Bible talks about "fellowship" it means "face-to-face" interaction. The theme of incarnation and the idea that the soul is expressed through the physical body (as opposed to text) are very apparent. The article concludes that Jesus probably would not tweet based on these shortcomings.

I appreciate the arguments. I find them full of great questions and concerns. I also find them a bit misguided and shortsighted.

The writer's presumption is that a primary purpose of the weekend gathering of believers is *community,* which in the context of the article means audible interactive communication or fellowship that is face-to-face. If this is the goal of weekend gatherings, then churches need to make a lot of adjustments. By this definition there is no community listening to a speaker for thirty minutes or more; there is no community watching people sing on a stage; there is no community watching videos, dramas, and so on.

In worship or any context, I'm a fan of good communication. As such, I'm a fan of face-to-face communication. I don't think my marriage would last forever if we never got to see each other, never got to date, or never got to sip wine together and talk late at night. In many situations face-to-face communication is preferred. However, the notion that Social Networking is not real community because it is not face-to-face is lacking.

This sort of an examination begs a deeper question: "What is real community in the first place?"

The Ideal Community

We lived in an amazing community in California. By that I mean everything you probably think of when I say the word *community*. It was beautiful. Parents were involved in the schools, and the schools were safe. The climate was amazing. Our home was always open to friends. Oftentimes we would come home and find we had guests in our pool because they felt so welcome. Neighbors watched out for one another's children. The church was growing and vibrant and exciting and making a difference in the town.

Doing ministry in Folsom, California, was exciting and challenging. The biggest challenge for me was figuring out how to be me in a town full of so many different groups of people. There was a community of poor people who had lived there for some time, and there was a community of very wealthy people associated with new industry. You could visibly see the difference by driving down School Street in the old neighborhood and then driving up the hill toward El Dorado Hills where a new housing development sprung up every week it seemed. When I use *community* here, I mean a particular financial class of people.

It was also challenging because I didn't always know my place with the various cliques of people. I'm not a jock, but a large portion of the men played golf regularly and went to basketball games. Many of them liked to do things like coach soccer and work out at the gym. I found myself praying that God would give me an interest in some sport and make me coordinated so I could connect with this community that I wasn't prone to attach myself to. When I use *community* here, I mean to describe a particular interest group.

Even with the challenges, it was a phenomenal experience and a great chapter of our lives. Part of it was because of a small group of friends that met in our home regularly for Bible study, good conversation, and a lot of fun. The relationships in the group were tight. People had one another's backs. People felt loved.

It was a close-knit community. When I say *community* this time, I mean it in the way that most people envision how they would like relationships to be in their church community. It was pretty special.

We use the word *community* to mean different things in different contexts. To be clear, when people in the church have issues and concerns with the community aspect of Social Networking, they are using the word in the sense I used to describe my small group.

I am sure there were other groups like mine. It was a big church. Some were enjoying the same kind of affinity and relationship with people as our group of twelve or fourteen. But if I am completely honest, I think those groups, as well as mine, were in the very small minority. Our small-group pastor had to fight to keep small groups going. On many occasions he had to work up a sweat to justify his job because people weren't "getting it" like "some of the groups were."

So, what made our group successful? My wonderful teaching? I don't think so, although they told me they liked it. The books we were reading at any given time? Nope. Some were dull and painful. Simply, we liked one another. It was fun. We had good interaction and banter. We were at similar stages in life. We were like-minded in our approach to our role in the Kingdom. We shared good advice with one another and remained transparent with our marriages and parental skills. We were all about the same age. We had similar tastes. And we worked hard at our relationships.

The groups that were struggling in our church were missing a lot of the above components. Some of them had good teachers, good books, and decent conversation. But they weren't thriving communities.

Sometimes the disconnect in our church small groups was also because of a conflict in our previous definitions of *community*—financial status; the part of town people were from; people's interests and tastes.

A Different Brand of Community

As stated, it's been suggested that real community is something that happens face-to-face. However, we know being face-to-face doesn't guarantee the interaction and affinity that we desire in community. Is it possible there is a new kind of community emerging?

Is it possible this new kind of community can actually bridge some of the gaps and remove some of the barriers we find in face-to-face community? Can that new community actually be superior in some ways to the disjointed and forced community some experienced in their small groups at my church?

I am friends with a good number of people on Facebook. Sometimes I get posts from people I don't immediately recognize, and I have to remind myself who they are. In those instances, it's usually the friend of a friend. Sometimes the person I don't readily recognize is from a previous church experience, part of a larger group I've met at conferences, or part of the creative networks I belong to. Sometimes the person I don't immediately recognize is from high school or college.

In all of those groups or communities of people, I can guarantee you there are some I wouldn't hang out with if they lived next door to me. We have nothing in common. I don't even remember hanging out with them when we were living in the same area years before. But we have that experience in common, and that is good enough in the Social Networking world.

I love these fringe connections. Showing all my cards, I am friends with people on Facebook who I never would have been friends with in high school. Maybe I thought I was too cool for them. Maybe I thought they were too cool for me. But in my Facebook world there are no geeks, jocks, stoners, punkers, or mathletes. Well, there are, but it isn't a problem or a deterrent from having conversation.

Scott was a major party guy in high school. I was a casual acquaintance of his. I'm sure I gave off the religious vibe a bit much for his liking. Scott is now forty-three and has questions about God. Guess who friended me on Facebook?

Tom was a high school nerd. I don't think I was very nice to him. As a matter of fact, I remember apologizing to him my senior year. I've always felt guilty about how I treated him. Guess who looked me up on Facebook and has regular conversation with me now?

Drew hates God. He distanced himself from me a few years back. I'm sure he was partly embarrassed because we used to go to church together. For years I tried to get together with him to talk, but to no avail. Last year he contacted me. It's a long, slow process, but we are talking once again about spiritual things.

Geeks, jocks, nerds, ne'er-do-wells, cheerleaders, foreigners, Christians, gays, geniuses, stoners, punkers, rich, and poor are all my friends. Really. We are honest with one another. We share stories. We encourage one another. We pray for one another. We ask questions of one another about life and God. I honestly don't know where we would have these conversations if we lived in the same town, which we don't. And it would never happen anyway.

I don't know that we ever did before—not in that other lifetime, not with the pressure we once had to conform to the rules of our particular clique. The cyber-high school passing period has gone to a whole new level. I now pass the same people in the halls, but these days we talk. We are getting to know one another. We talk about the old times, and those times give us the framework for new conversation. It's a giant high school—the groups are diverse—but nobody is getting stuffed in a garbage can or a toilet after school.

Post: Closing Walls and Ticking Clocks

What Is Behind the Question of Distraction?

My parents gave me a book called *Der Struwwelpeter* (Shaggy Peter). It was written in 1845 and every page is thick cardboard. The book has been passed down through generations in our German family. It is a collection of stories designed to teach children lessons. The title of the book comes from the first story, which is about a boy with improper grooming and consequently other children don't like him.

It's written in German. When I was a child it scared me (or maybe scarred me?). I couldn't read it, but the pictures were horrible. Images of a boy getting his thumbs cut off (because he sucked them), a girl burning to death with her cats crying as they watched (because she played with matches), and a man drowning white children in ink (because they teased black children) are burned in my memory.

One story is called "Die Geschichte von Hans Guck-in-die-Luft" (The Story of Johnny Head-in-Air). It's about a boy who fails to watch where he is walking. He's always distracted. The clouds, the sky, and the birds are all distracters. He falls in the river at the end and learns his lesson because the worst possible thing has happened to him—he's lost his book. At least they didn't hack his legs off.

I get that the big lesson is for Johnny to pay attention to his surroundings. But in a storybook where huge scissors cut off thumbs and little girls with pigtails are charred in front of their cats, I'd at least expect Johnny to step on a land mine. Instead, he loses his book—the technology of the times and the key to Johnny's future as an educated young man.

If the story were written today, I wonder what Johnny would lose? His phone? His laptop? His Kindle? Maybe the story wouldn't be written because his technology would be the very thing distracting him. Maybe today he would be checking his Twitter feed as he fell into the subway train trench.

"I don't like that youth pastor one bit," said my friend about the youth pastor at his church. "That kid always has his damn nose buried in his text messages and Twitters. Every time I talk to him he is looking down." I understand my friend's sentiments. The other day I almost hit a text-walker who stepped off the curb in front of my Jeep. Texting and walking might become the new drinking and driving.

My friend pastors at a church where they have a Social Networking ban in their offices. If you are caught using Facebook during work hours, you will be fired. His boss decreed, "We are here to equip people to do the work of the ministry and need to minimize distractions."

One gentleman in our church had his smartphone in his hand during a sermon when he was visiting his mom and dad's church over college break. A woman tapped him on the shoulder and told him he was being distracting to everyone around him. Then she added, "You should pay attention to the sermon, Son." (He was reading his YouVersion Bible on his phone.)

Oftentimes people will be outspoken about their lack of desire to join Social Networking platforms because of the banality of the conversation. "I don't need to know about you waking up at 3:00 a.m. with diarrhea." "Who cares what you had for dinner?" "Great. You hate your cable company."

At the root of this sentiment is a belief that shallow conversation is a distraction that keeps us from important things and that needs to be challenged on one level. However, the problem with technology-related distraction is legitimate. It is also multilayered and complex. We cannot address the issue of distraction without peeling the onion.

Defining Distraction

What do we mean when we use the word *distraction*? By definition, a distraction is something that takes our attention away from what it should be focused on. Or it is something that divides our attention.

But what are we being distracted from? Probably a million things. It's all a matter of opinion. If a husband and wife have a conversation while he is watching the proverbial football game, he probably thinks she is a distraction, whereas she thinks the game is a distraction.

In order to define distractions we have to first define what is important to us and what should be holding our attention.

We will always have conversations with one another about our perceptions of how we are each distracted. This is not a problem of technology. This is a human problem.

Some hear a story like "Johnny Head-in-Air" and say it's still a good lesson and our children need to know the value of reading rather than being distracted by video games and the Internet and Social Networking. I'll admit it's an attractive trade from a parent's perspective. Most of the time I'd rather see my children with their heads in a book than with a game controller in their hands. But can we say it's a fair trade in every circumstance?

A concerned mom came and talked to me in my office about her daughter. Her daughter had no friends. She never went out to parties or sleepovers. She didn't like to play in the neighborhood. She was getting obese from lack of exercise. All she wanted to do was read books. "Johnny Head-in-Air" could have easily been written "Johnny Head-in-Book."

If we wanted to demonize the book as something that distracts us from what we should be doing, we could have a pretty good case. The book keeps us in seclusion. The book keeps us from socializing and sharpening our conversation skills. The book takes up a lot of our time that could be spent on things that make a difference. The book is full of crazy ideas that mess with our thinking.

The book is an old technology that has maintained its form as well as taken on new forms as it is recast and melded with other technologies and their counterparts. The Internet, hypertext links, e-books, and any number of digital devices from the smartphone to e-readers like the Kindle and the Nook have forever changed the way we read books. A book, no matter what form it comes in, is not inherently a distracter. The potential for distraction lies with me, the reader.

When we define what is important to us, any number of things can fit within the framework of our goals and vision. Technology does not need to be a distraction when we identify our intentions and what we want to accomplish. It might fit perfectly. If we think creatively and resourcefully, we might even harness it for accomplishing the very goals we set out after. And when we allow for downtime, recreation, and a healthy dose of shallow things, we might find it isn't a distraction even if it doesn't line up perfectly with the things we do to accomplish the things we want.

If we have a problem with Social Networking distractions, it is a signpost for us that there is a deeper problem. Most likely, we have other distractions. Most likely, we need to look at our priorities.

Real Distractions

I don't want to give Social Networking an easy out by putting the entire burden on us. Yes, distractions are ultimately our problem to fix, but every distracter comes with its own set of lures.

I drink alcohol. I have no problem with it from a biblical perspective. My father is an alcoholic who has been dry for almost two decades. Alcoholism is my dad's problem. Not mine. I like a good scotch. Alcohol is one of many beverages I enjoy, including soda and coffee. However, alcohol presents a problem for my dad that soda does not. Even though it is not inherently an evil beverage, it contains an alluring substance that numbs his particular demons for a short time before causing huge problems. He needs to not drink booze. It is a distracter.

We all have addictions or a propensity to certain kinds of addictions and distractions. Some of those can only be managed by staying completely away from the substance or thing that we are addicted to or distracted by. Some addictions and distractions can be managed.

Social Networking carries with it some potential for certain kinds of distractions. When people say, "I don't need the distraction of Social Networking," they might be referring to these potential issues:

- Compulsiveness. For the person who has to look at her smartphone every time a message of some kind flashes on the screen, or the person who does not know how to rest, Social Networking could be a potential distracter.

- Isolation. For the person who excludes himself from physical interaction, Social Networking has the potential for aiding and abetting the loner.

- Escapism. For the person who has a penchant for losing herself in any activity in order to cope with, deny, or forget her circumstances, Social Networking presents risks.

- Pornography. Social Networking has the potential for the exchange of sexually explicit messages and links to pornographic material.

- Narcissism. For the person who loves to talk about himself to the exclusion of others, enjoys attention, or loves self-promotion, Social Networking can be a great platform for him to fall in love with himself in a whole new way. (Hang tight. We'll devote more time to this one later.)

We need to make sure, however, that we don't vilify Social Networking even with these built-in potentials. As with many things, Social Networking can be useful or harmful depending on the user and the safeguards that are put in place.

Each one of these potential problems can be avoided in the world of Social Networking. For instance, preferences can be set so that one has to actually log on to the network in order to update or read updates rather than receive a text, alert, or e-mail message each time there is activity. Preferences can be set so that each person who wants to view a profile or follow a person must first be approved.

As to the potential problems that the technologies' preference settings cannot help an individual with, such as self-control and tendencies to isolate oneself, the responsibility lies with the individual to know himself or herself, ask for help, practice open communication, and allow others to edit her or him.

Parents who see these tendencies in their children don't necessarily need to ban a child from using new technologies. Rather, they can use the technologies as teachable moments and opportunities to converse with their children about how to deal with real problems in a real world.

It is becoming more and more the norm that classrooms incorporate Social Networking platforms as part of a child's education. Chatrooms, Facebook pages, and interactive blackboards are being used in middle schools, high schools, and colleges.

The potential for distraction is inherent in any external source. Internal sources and a lack of safeguards are what unleash the beast of distraction.

What Is Behind the Question of Time?

According to the Nielsen Company in its 2010 report *Internet & Social Media Consumer Insights,* the amount of time Internet users spent on Social Networking sites doubled from 2009 to 2010. Between 2008 and 2010, Twitter users grew by more than 1,500 percent. Twenty-two percent of time spent online in the United States is attributed to Social Networking sites. Fifty-five percent of United States Internet households have at least one or more Social Network profiles.

eMarketer.com referenced a helpful report in 2010 in its online article "Two-Thirds of Web Users to Visit Soc Nets in 2014" (www.emarketer.com/Article.aspx?R=1007712) by sharing the following statistics and quotations from Debra Aho Williamson, senior analyst for eMarketer.com and author of the report *Social Network Demographics and Usage:*

> Usage of social networking sites rose sharply in 2009, thanks to the ever-increasing popularity of Facebook. eMarketer estimates that 57.5% of Internet users...will use a social network at least once a month in 2010....

> "There is no doubt anymore that social networks...are an essential part of the Internet experience."...

> By 2014, nearly two-thirds of all Internet users...will be regular users of social networks...."Teens and young adults are old news....This year, 60% of Internet users ages 35 to 44 and one-half of those in the 45-to-54 age group will use social networks at least once a month."

The article goes on to say that these changes will continue to grow and that by 2014, the use of Social Networks by the upper age brackets will have increased significantly. More than half of those fifty-five to sixty-four years old will regularly use a Social Networking site. This will be up from 34.3 percent in 2009. The senior group (sixty-five and up) is expected to reach 37.9 percent usage in 2014, up from 14.1 percent in 2009.

Other reports estimated that the average Internet user spent more than six hours a month on Social Networking sites. Overall time spent on the Internet in 2010, according to comScore Data Mine, was more than thirty hours a month, and persons between the ages of forty-five and fifty-four "set the high bar averaging more than thirty-nine hours online each month." Most studies show that the time devoted to Internet use is on the increase as well as that of Social Networking, which now accounts for more than 25 percent of Americans' time online. Other studies show time spent in Social Networking to be second only to time spent on Google, a search engine.

The question of time is a very close kin to the question of distraction. Educators have increasingly voiced concerns about students being distracted from studies in and out of the classroom and spending their time wisely.

On the flip side, some educators look at Social Networking from a different perspective—seeing its potential to sharpen minds, enhance relational and social skills, and give students a welcome distraction from the normal stresses at home and at school. Bernhard Warner is a journalist, media consultant, and university lecturer. His article "Is Social Networking a Waste of Time?" in the *Times Online* states:

> I admire the growing number of young students who dedicate hours to designing complicated widgets and applications too. Yes, they're probably neglecting their history paper to complete it, but the end product is a far more valuable lesson learned in creativity, courage and computer coding. When I look at all the creativity, the collaboration and the activism being generated in these networks, I am hopeful for the future. Perhaps it is we educators who need to learn how to harness this power into our everyday classroom lessons.

Parents have concerns about how their children spend their time at home as well as at school. When I was a boy my parents went through a phase where they threw away the television (actually threw it on a bonfire) and forbade us from watching TV at friends' homes. We were allowed to read the Bible or approved books and enjoy God's green earth for recreation.

I remember one of my dad's favorite songs during this time of his greatest religious piety and pendulum swing away from all things "of the world" in favor of all things right and pure. He would repeat the chorus to the John Prine song "Spanish Pipedream" over and over: "Blow up your TV, throw away your paper....Try an' find Jesus on your own." Later in life I found myself actually buying that song and listening to all the words out of curiosity, only to find it was about a drunken soldier who ends up marrying a topless dancer he met in a bar as they were both looking for an escape. God bless you, Dad.

My parents went through a phase of life where they decided we were spending too much time on things that didn't matter. What mattered to them were family, God, friends, and enjoying the simple things of life. Not bad values by any stretch of the imagination. However, their execution of instilling these values was less than desirable for me and has had ripple effects on our family today. It has been hard at various times throughout my life to separate ideas about and toward God from the strict rules that were imposed not only by my parents but by the church we went to as well.

The record albums were the second things to go. All were burned except the ones I gave to my girlfriend, who protected them until I married her at a later date. I remember the incident that created our own personal *Bonfire of the Vanities*. I was in my room listening to the Steve Miller Band when my dad shouted, "Turn off that damn music and get out here for family Bible reading!"—a classic newly converted move by my dad that lives in Voelz home infamy.

My parents didn't teach us how to manage our time with this initial reactionary experiment, which lasted for maybe three years. They instead taught us that the only way to live a life of time well spent was to deny there was a world around us and abstain from every possible time-robbing potential and "appearance of evil."

The phrase "appearance of evil" (KJV) is found in the same passage as another phrase that was often quoted around our church: "Warn those who are idle and disruptive." Funny, the phrase "idle and disruptive" is the NIV rendering of the KJV "unruly." However, our pastor saw fit to use two translations together to shape his personal philosophy. In his mind, warning the idle and staying away from the potential of evil clearly translated into, "Don't watch TV or go to movies."

Abstaining from every "appearance of evil" in my parent's KJV tradition coupled with "warn the idle" were the mottos for a slippery path of legalism. The 1 Thessalonians passage that contains the phrases in question is within the context of interpersonal relationships as well as public worship:

> Now we ask you, brothers and sisters, to acknowledge those who work hard among you, who care for you in the Lord and who admonish you. Hold them in the highest regard in love because of their work. Live in peace with each other. And we urge you, brothers and sisters, warn those who are idle and disruptive, encourage the disheartened, help the weak, be patient with everyone. Make sure that nobody pays back wrong for wrong, but always strive to do what is good for each other and for everyone else.
>
> Rejoice always, pray continually, give thanks in all circumstances; for this is God's will for you in Christ Jesus.
>
> Do not put out the Spirit's fire. Do not treat prophecies with contempt but test them all; hold on to what is good, reject whatever is harmful. (1 Thessalonians 5:12-22 TNIV®)

The context here is living in peace and harmony with one another as you listen to God and respond to him in community. The idle are those who do nothing to encourage the disheartened, help the weak, or be patient with everyone. The idle are not proactive about working out peace. They react to one another harshly and refuse to be held accountable.

The phrase "rejoice always" begins a salutation that speaks specifically to corporate worship and how we listen to the Spirit together, test prophetic words, and stay away from those words that do not match up or that fail the test of true prophecy, including, but not limited to, Paul's test in 1 Corinthians 14:4 that prophecy should build up, strengthen, or edify the body.

Avoiding prophecies that are clearly evil and avoiding things that might have the potential for evil are two different things. Paul was not giving the Thessalonians license to decide what might be evil according to personal opinion.

Time is a precious commodity. Once it is gone, it is gone for good. You can't get it back. As horrible as the experience of the ascetic lifestyle was for us boys, I appreciate my parents' attempts. I appreciate that they tried a different approach with SpanishPipedream 2.0, which was to let the TV back in the house but keep it in the closet until it was time to watch it.

Unfortunately, my parents' methods (they have since repented) and similar methods are still popular today. Maybe they aren't as harsh, but complete abstinence from technology is a popular methodology with some households. I live close to Amish country; you would understand very quickly what I mean on a drive (or gallop) through some towns around me.

Identifying what is important to us and managing our time wisely are important and valiant practices. However, denial, asceticism, angry reactions, and demonization of things that are neither good nor evil can have lasting and damaging effects on children and adults who are learning to exist in a continually reimagined new world.

At the root of the time concern regarding Social Networking lies fear of change and of losing valued traditions; distrust of ourselves and of anything that makes new promises to enhance our lives; a lack of understanding of how to manage time in a new venue; and perhaps, as in the case of my early church experience, a legalistic and slippery view of scripture. Some of these things are very big issues that can only be resolved from the inside out. By taking the time to ask a few questions and educate ourselves, some might be prevented.

To be fair, the whole context of scripture does in fact give warnings about how we spend our time. Sloth is recognized as one of the seven deadly sins in Catholicism. This is based on more than one passage. Only you and those around you whom you trust and have invited to edit you can help you determine those warnings.

Is Social Networking a waste of time? For some, absolutely yes. So is staying four hours at an all-you-can-eat buffet while trying heaping helpings of the forty food groups it offers. So is too much reading. So is too much time volunteering to the detriment of your family.

Conclusion

The questions surrounding the Christian's responsibility in the world, as the church, and to the church are questions about mission. Oftentimes, technologies and inanimate objects become the target of the church's angst and an easy scapegoat on which we can lay our deficiencies that keep us from our mission—that is to say, Jesus' mission.

What am I doing to make a difference? How am I sharing the hope of the gospel? Am I practicing charity and hospitality? Am I sharing my own personal redemption stories and pointing people to Christ? Am I investing in people? Am I fostering relationship? Am I investigating ways to harness new technologies for the sake of the Kingdom? Do I spend more time standing for the things I know to be true or standing against things that could potentially affect me?

These are right questions. Keep asking them. Keep investigating new technologies in light of the questions above. Having good answers to the questions above will keep moving you forward as you are faithful to Jesus' mission.

Finally, as we are answering these questions, consider how the mission of Jesus isn't a destination. We don't arrive at the mission. We participate in the mission. High school isn't all about the diploma or the classes we move to and from. It's about life experience. It's about the passing periods, the relationships and rhythms of life that demand our attention on the way to class. It's what happens on the bus ride to and from. Kingdom projects, dreams, and goals are all valiant, but making disciples and teaching them to protect and value everything he offers us (Matthew 28:19-20) is something that happens along the way.

Post: Fear Not

Growing Up Blind

When I was young we lived on ten acres two miles in from the highway on a dirt road. It was a country boy's paradise. My mom and dad allowed our friends and us to shoot guns, ride dirt bikes at breakneck speeds, swim in the creek without life jackets, and roam hundreds of acres that didn't belong to us. We were gone for hours at a time with no freedom-inhibiting cell phone calls from Mom.

We felt completely safe. My mom and dad had normal parental anxiety about our safety, but they also felt we lived in a relatively safe world. They knew there were unsafe places in the world, but those places were far removed from us.

Other than a looming fear that Russia was going to nuke us, Americans once felt impervious to the idea of any war or terrorist attack on our soil. Even the threat of personal assault seemed unlikely. The evening news brought us details of the Iran hostage crisis, the Iran-Contra affair, Jim Jones and the mass suicides in Guyana, U.S. embassy bombings in Beirut, and the assassination of Egyptian president Anwar Sadat. Things happened "over there."

Sure, we had crazies like Charlie Manson and the guy who shot John Lennon, but parents tucked their children in at night assuring them that bad things happened in other countries or in the big bad cities.

As children, the greatest technological advances we experienced in our homes were phones with buttons, an oven that cooked our food in seconds, and video games we could play on our own television.

On the one hand, the world does not seem as safe as when I was a boy. But on the other hand, have things really gotten worse?

Fearing Technology

I was in the bank last week when a woman yelled at the teller because there was an error in her account, which she had seen in her monthly printed and mailed statement. The teller kindly told the woman, "Ma'am, we can get you signed up for Internet banking and you can monitor this online." The woman screamed back, "I don't let a machine do my banking! What's this world coming to?"

I assume she was afraid of a few things. She may not have known how to use the technology. She might not trust the technology to not make mistakes. She most likely grew up with the idea that banking and bankers are personal and human. None of these fears or concerns is outrageous.

In the mid-1990s, *Saturday Night Live* did a spoof commercial for a company called "Old Glory Insurance." The commercial began with a group of older women sitting and talking about their fears of gangs and rap music and the things that made them feel insecure, such as robots. Sam Waterston of the TV series *Law & Order* was the company spokesman in the commercial:

> I'm Sam Waterston of the popular TV series *Law & Order*. As a senior citizen, you're probably aware of the threat robots pose. Robots are everywhere, and they eat old people's medicine for fuel. Well now there's a company that offers coverage against the unfortunate event of a robot attack—Old Glory Insurance. Old Glory will cover you with no health checkup or age consideration. You need to feel safe. And that's harder and harder to do nowadays because robots may strike at any time.

It's one of the funniest spoof commercials I've ever seen on *SNL*. While writing this, I paused to watch it twice on YouTube.

I used to joke about my poor grandma not setting her VCR or any of the digital clocks on her appliances. My grandma saw more technological advances in her lifetime than she could have ever dreamed, and they caught her by surprise. The learning curve was steep for Grandma. Technology didn't scare her; it made her nervous and frustrated, and it sometimes made her feel stupid.

I'm sure some older adults fear robots. But I don't think it's just an older person's dilemma. The fear of technology taking over and humanity losing control is a popular motif in science fiction, and has been for years. The *Terminator* franchise of movies that began in the late 1980s continues to fascinate sci-fi fans with titles like *Rise of the Machines* and 2009's *Salvation*, which portrays the battle against technology as being far from over. From 2004 to 2009 the Syfy channel resurrected and reimagined the popular 1970s TV show *Battlestar Galactica*, wherein once again an epic battle is recast in a new plot with a familiar underlying theme of humankind battling the very beast it created.

In a genre rich with the plot of humans versus technology, Stanley Kubrick's *2001: A Space Odyssey* is one of the greatest and most respected illustrations of humankind's confrontation with the fear of technology. Kubrick's film chronicles the evolution of human beings, their creation of tools, and the subsequent takeover by the tools they created in the first place—specifically, the takeover of a sabotaging onboard spaceship computer named HAL. Although the plot seems like something that would sell well as a Michael Bay movie today, it was written in 1968.

Plato's *Phaedrus* contains Socrates' scolding of print, citing that print has the power to destroy our memories and turn us inward. Socrates also argued that print would destroy communities and common places where individuals share stories and learn from one another. You are now reading a book. If Socrates had his way, writing would have ceased post-370 B.C.

In the early nineteenth century, the Luddites—a group of British textile workers—destroyed looms and machinery as an act of defiance against the Industrial Revolution. They vandalized not only to keep their jobs, but also to oppose the crime against humanity that they believed was happening. As machines and unskilled workers replaced the skilled artisans, the Luddites imagined and feared an unproductive, slothful, mechanical, and less human world.

Neo-Luddism carries on in this tradition and demonizes any new technology that threatens a simple ascetic life. It proposes a return to the way things used to be—whenever that was.

The fear of technology and how it has the power to control us, make us less human, and destroy us (be it physically or mentally) has been around for a while.

Fearing What Might Happen to Us or Our Loved Ones

Today, I am sitting in an airport in Nashville. I am chatting via text messaging with a friend in California. My Facebook page is open, and I'm reading posts from friends. My Twitter account is logged on. CNN is on the airport television. In the ten minutes that I've been sitting here, I've learned of the untimely death of a young pop musician, who died from an overdose; a mother who is on the run after allegedly killing her children; tornado warnings across the state; a terrorist ring interruption; and unrest in multiple countries, including terrorist activity in Norway.

This kind of heartache happens every day all over the world. Yet because of advances in technology and a variety of news streams at our fingertips and within earshot, we hear everyone's bad news from everywhere in real time.

One hundred years ago, our main news resources were newspapers, pamphlets, and word of mouth. Televisions were not in our homes. Radios were not personal possessions, and even amateur radio broadcasts for the few who owned two-way radios were restricted to short ranges. In 1917, radio broadcasts became illegal for individuals and were the prerogative of the U.S. government as the country entered World War I.

Children have always been sold into slavery. People have always been murdered in the streets. Countries have always been invaded. Women have always been taken advantage of. Families have always been at risk. "The LORD said [to Cain], 'What did you do? The voice of your brother's blood is crying to me from the ground'" (Genesis 4:10).

Social Networking has the same inherent risks we take every day by walking down the street, going to the mall, going to church, or eating out. We don't know who is watching us, overhearing us, following us, or planning harm for us (if anyone is doing any of those things at all). These risks are real and unpredictable but shouldn't paralyze us.

The Hyperbolic Media

When it comes to Social Networking, mainstream media hype and sensationalism along with a rapid transfer of new information and real-time alerts of global tragedy have tainted us.

There are indeed risks that exist online. And yes, it's true that before we got in the habit of sharing details online, these risks did not exist in the same way that they do now. But quite frankly, these risks exist outside of any participation in Social Networking activity.

Identity theft, embarrassing situations, slander, surveillance, photos, addresses and former addresses, credit history, court records, and opinions about us are all potentially found online regardless of our participation in Social Networking. Information about ourselves is more and more present online whether or not we post the information.

This is the world we live in, and the best we can do is manage the risks without letting it consume us. The mainstream media have made a business out of sensationalizing the risks for profit and ratings. It's their business. It's their advertiser's business.

The mainstream media often personify the Web as an all-knowing, unforgiving stalker. It's "Big Brother is watching you" all over again. But the truth is that most of the information about yourself that is available online is not accessible to everyone by doing an easy Google search and not as many people frequent your blog and look at your photos as you might think.

Mainstream media also perpetuate risks. For example, when a female pop star posts a picture of herself online being mildly naughty, we hear about it right away. The media do not let it die. "How could she do this?" "Doesn't she know young girls look to her as an example?" "What kind of parent allows this?" Parents will often hear these stories and make rash decisions about allowing their children to use Social Media because of the risk of ruining a reputation. The message the media sends is, "Young girls everywhere are posting naughty pictures on Social Networking sites," which quickly is translated into, "Keep your children off the Internet."

What the mainstream media fail to do is talk about the fact that the person in question is a celebrity. The negative fallout and the risks to celebrities and politicians who make mistakes have always been heightened. The cyber risks are disproportional to the average person. Just ask Sarah Palin.

The mainstream media fail to mention the unrealistic likelihood of this happening to our own daughters. They fail to mention that everyone makes mistakes, and they plant disdain in the public's minds. They fail to mention how we might educate our own children about making decisions regarding sexuality. And they fail to recognize that if they just left these things alone, they would dissipate.

As a matter of fact, sharing details about ourselves online—warts and all—might help us be more understanding and forgiving. When

I say something online that I wish I could take back, it teaches me to be more careful. It teaches me to manage my emotions. And it also lets people see that I am human. We all make mistakes.

I am not suggesting that there are no risks in online activity. I hope I have been clear about that. However, I *am* suggesting that the risks are a lot smaller than *The View* or your local news correspondent may let on. And I am suggesting that the mainstream media does an inadequate job of informing the general public about the joys and triumphs of Social Networking. Good news doesn't sell.

There are many sites that give great information about reducing risks online for you and your loved ones. I won't list them all here. Most of the guidelines fall under the category of common sense and accountability. I'll also suggest that most risks to children can be avoided by parental involvement and monitoring of online activity.

A lot of parents are afraid their children will disrespect them or think they don't trust them if they don't allow them online privacy, but safety is not a matter of trust. Peeking at your child's diary may or may not be a breach of trust. When your child's diary is online, the rules change. If your child puts it online, she or he is not being private with information in the first place. You are the parent. Be one.

The Disproportionate Media

The mainstream media also skews our views and aids our fears by not providing a sufficient counterweight to the bad stories it tells. Any good news reporter knows that death tolls and scandals are what steal the breaking news updates in the eleven o'clock spot. In the words of Don Henley, "We love dirty laundry."

As such, the stories that are hopeful, if they get told at all, are usually reserved for early time slots or are released in an online format only. Occasionally one or two of the Social Networking victory stories will sneak through, especially if it benefits the news source.

On March 11, 2011, an earthquake and a follow-up tsunami devastated Japan. A concerned woman by the name of Megan Walsh sent a desperate Twitter message to the *Today Show*'s Ann Curry as Ann was being sent to Japan to cover the story. Megan told Ann that her sister, Canon Purdy, was missing and to please send updates about evacuees. Ann replied, "I will do my best."

Curry obtained a photograph of Purdy and was able to visit the middle school at which Purdy taught. It was still standing and was being used as an evacuation center. A few minutes after arriving, Purdy was located and used Curry's phone to call her family in San Francisco to tell them she was okay.

In February of 2011, a project called "Unheard in New York" put cell phones into the hands of many homeless people. Fifty-eight-year-old Daniel Morales, a homeless man who benefited from the project, joined Twitter. One tweet reunited him with his daughter Sarah, whom he had not seen in eleven years.

These stories are larger than life and don't happen every day with this kind of drama and magnitude. But what are even better are the stories of redemption, repaired relationships, fulfilled needs, and victory that will never reach the ears of the mainstream media because they lack the kind of drama that keeps advertisers interested—and quite frankly, us as well.

The local news affiliate may not be interested in our small-scale stories. But what would happen if we started using Social Networking as the vehicle through which we shared redemption stories? What if we told them around the bonfire? In our homes? At our churches? In the coffee shops?

Imagined Fears

When I was a boy, some people in my church had a rock-and-roll vendetta. They, like many of the people I grew up with in church, spent most of their time investigating the ills of society. They felt it was their duty to watch movies, listen to music, and scan for sin. Once they found something they could latch on to, they made it their soapbox. The particular soapbox that affected me was called "backmasking." (Backmasking is a recording technique in which a sound or message is recorded backward on to a track that is meant to be played forward. Various rock bands have been accused of inserting satanic messages into songs by using this technique.)

Larry was a youth pastor at the height of the backmasking scare. Many will never forget what he did one night at a youth group meeting with parents present. Larry told us all that backmasking was not the problem. Rock was not inherently evil. And parents needn't fear potential subconscious interpretations of messages. Larry told everyone that fear was ruling their hearts and that fear was not from God.

Larry went on to talk about perfect love casting out fear. He told stories of the angels appearing to people and first saying, "Fear not." He talked about seizing opportunities for the sake of the Kingdom. He told parents that they needed to stop searching down rabbit holes for the things that might be destroying our youth and learn to talk things through with their children.

Larry taught, "The problem is not what may or may not be on a record when you play it backward. The problem is being unwilling to talk with our children about what is heard in any genre of music when we play it forward. The problem is not rock music. The problem is parents being disinterested in their children and not being attuned to their children's pain or listening to their questions about life. The answer is not to burn albums and books. The answer is giving our children the tools they need to discern what is godly and healthy. The answer is not to hide. The answer is to face fear, call it out, and educate."

Larry went on to tell the story of how he was "saved" at a Christian rock concert. He shared many more stories about how music was changing the life of youth for good. He talked about concerts that were raising money for charity. He talked about rock stars who were paying more attention to a hurting world than the church was.

Until that night, no one had heard the redemption stories and opportunities Larry presented. They always existed, but they were drowned out by the noise of a more popular crowd that shouted, "Kill the beast!"

Post: Not-So-Stranger Danger

Real Dangers

Relationships are risky. Period. In relationship there is potential to experience pain, frustration, discouragement, and betrayal. But the reason we take the risk is because relationships also provide potential for joy, fulfillment, shared experience, growth, and love.

In the world of Social Networking, the biggest risks are relational. Although Social Networking may put a different spin on an old relational problem, we'd be hard-pressed to say it creates the problem.

Cyberbullying

There are some risks that exist online over which we have little influence. However, these risks exist in more venues than a parent could possibly control. The answer to managing these risks is not to abandon the technology that houses the risks. The answer is good communication with our children that gives them the tools they need to survive in a changing world.

One such risk is cyberbullying. Cyberbullying is in a class by itself when it comes to Social Networking risks because we can only influence and teach our children about it, as opposed to adding a filter to it. Even if our children do not engage in cyberbullying, we cannot guarantee they will not be bullied.

Cyberbullying is often the result of a gag, peer pressure, or a dare. Oftentimes the recipient did nothing to deserve the bullying.

Although bullying has often been associated with an ongoing aggression toward another, as in the case of the proverbial school bully who is big and mean and makes other boys and girls give up their lunch money, cyberbullying can be just as devastating for a person and can come from someone who poses no physical threat.

The proverbial school bully is usually pictured as a tough male who got held back a few grades and resents it, so he takes it out on the little pimple-faced boy whose dad drove him to school in a fancy car. Now, the bully has become a sweet little girl who feels a power online that she doesn't possess in real life combined with little risk of being sent to the principal's office or getting in trouble at all.

In other words, Social Networking becomes the great equalizer. Although stripping social barriers has many positive implications for ministry, cyberbullying is the other side of the gift card. Little Suzy may be all pigtails and giggles in person, but she has potential to be your worst nightmare online.

Not to mention, sometimes cyberbullying comes in the form of anonymous taunts if the networking is being done in chatrooms or sites where one does not have to leave any identification, for example, on blogs or YouTube posts.

There are a few easy things we can do to lessen the risk of cyberbullying and negative talk in Social Networking platforms. Just like we had to learn how to deal with the schoolyard bully (walk a different way to school; always walk in pairs; report it to the principal), we need to understand how to prevent pushing around on this new playground.

When MySpace hit the Internet, our then seventeen-year-old daughter got an account. We monitored the account, as was our habit with our children's online activity. One thing we noticed very quickly was that the "cool" boys and girls were the ones who had the most online friends. These "friends" were not always people the teens knew.

Some were acquaintances, some were friends of other friends, and some were added simply because someone asked them. The game quickly became "Who has the most friends?"

Being new to the idea of teenagers and the Internet, we let it go on for a bit while monitoring the situation. It quickly became apparent that allowing our daughter to add friends whom she did not know was a bad idea, even if they were friends of friends. Pornography, threats, and just plain meanness became the flies in the MySpace ointment that was on the family computer. We quickly put an end to it by having our daughter close her account and open a new one where she could only add friends she knew personally. We had to know of them as well. My daughter was required to explain to us how she knew any individual we asked about. The number of friends was limited, and questionable activity became a seldom occurrence.

Cyberbullying is not just a child's dilemma, though children certainly are at a greater risk than adults. Adults should be cautious about who they are adding as friends to their profiles. When relationships end, consider ending the online relationship as well. When jobs change, think about weeding out the friends with whom you no longer associate.

David met Joe at a church conference. They were in a talk-back session after the main speaker finished a presentation. The participants sat around tables. At their table there was a disagreement between David and Joe about the topic at hand, but it was nothing more than a little friendly fire. As has become the custom for many, everyone exchanged contact information at the end of the meeting.

The discussion-table conversation continued online following the conference. At first it was entirely friendly. However, one day Joe called David an unflattering name on Facebook. David blew him off, but Joe persisted. Soon Joe was posting feedback and comments on all of David's Facebook updates.

David "unfriended" Joe and blocked him from making further comments. Joe had become a cyberbully—an adult cyberbully.

Oftentimes, Christians believe it is not only their right but also their mission to call people out online who they deem to have done or to have said something unbiblical. When Rob Bell published his book *Love Wins* I thought the heavens might crack and smite the garbage-slinging perpetrators who made him their target (and I don't even believe smiting is something that's done).

Rob's ideas about the existence of hell ruffled quite a few feathers on the World Wide Web. A great majority of the lashing he took happened before the book was even released. That's right; before anyone read a word, speculation as to what he *might* be saying was enough to earn him the title of "heretic."

Few stopped to think that Rob is a real-life human being with real feelings. Regardless of what the book contains or whether Rob is right or wrong, he has a wife and children. And the Internet is worldwide.

Still, there was no shortage of people condemning Rob to the hell he questioned in his book; no shortage of name-calling; no shortage of hateful blog posts and video vendettas. There were even a few death threats.

I like to refer to this practice as "hanging the cyber BA"—blog assassination. The world has access to your blog. The people you are defaming have families. Blogs do not always give the accused an opportunity to respond to you and to everyone who has read your post.

Blog assassinations are irresponsible and wrong. I'm not talking about the kind of blog post where we say we didn't like a movie or a song or a philosophy or an idea. I am talking about character assassination—the kind of post that demeans or belittles a person in order to blow off steam. You don't have to have a personal Web address for your blog for it to count. Social Networking is often referred to as "microblogging." One hundred forty characters can sting just as much as a wordy manifesto.

Disagree online. Go ahead. Disagree strongly if you must. But disagree in a way that is helpful. One of the safeguards I often use for myself when disagreeing online is to ask myself a series of questions. You'd be surprised at how many comments going through this exercise reserves:

Do I think someone will be hurt unless I challenge him or her?

> Can I disagree in a way that doesn't drag the name of Jesus through the mud?

>> Do I really hold this opinion, or am I jumping on a bandwagon?

>>> Will my contrary opinion help someone or might it do more harm?

>>>> Can I state my opinion in a non-aggressive manner?

>>>> Do I have this other person's best interest at heart?

>>> Do I just want to win an argument?

>> Do I make myself look good by disagreeing, and is my motivation pride?

> Am I ready for a fight?

Did this person ask for my opinion?

If you are a blogger, consider removing the ability to make comments on your posts or set your parameters so you have to approve comments. If you post to any Social Media with networking capabilities, such as YouTube, consider doing the same.

At a bare minimum, if you invite comments from everyone, be ready to engage people in conversation in those platforms. Sometimes going the extra mile and engaging people in conversation are healing and promote mutual understanding. Sometimes you will find it is not worth it and some people just want to argue. It's just like the rest of life.

In ministry we have to live with the mantra "People are worth it." There will be times when we are stepped on and taken advantage of. Count on it. It doesn't mean we lie down and take a beating. It doesn't mean we don't set boundaries. But it does mean we will encounter an occasional bully with or without Social Networking.

Forget Big Brother; Your Boss Is Watching (Oh, and Jesus too)

If you have some time on your hands and perhaps a morbid curiosity, you might consider doing a Google search for "fired because of Social Networking." You'll come up with more than seven million results.

Stacey worked in a care facility for older adults. She loved her job. One day she took a picture of herself in one of the facility apartments. She wasn't a friend with her boss online, but he was a friend of a friend. Her boss ended up seeing the picture she had uploaded and recognized the apartment as one of his. In the background there were medications on the counter and a picture of the tenant on a shelf. Because of HIPAA laws protecting privacy, Stacey was fired.

True, few people may be reading your posts and tweets, but the probability of people seeing those same posts and tweets as they are commented on and reposted and re-tweeted is much higher.

Todd was a youth pastor. During a summer camp, one of the girls in the youth group posted, "I think my youth pastor is sexy." Todd should have left it alone or at least pulled someone in (like his wife) to talk to this girl about the awkwardness of the post. Instead, Todd commented on her post, "I know." Todd was being silly—and stupid.

Speculations started to rumble back at home. "What kind of a youth pastor talks about being sexy with a young girl?" "Did Todd mean that he knows he is sexy or that he knows she thinks he's sexy?" The fact is, Todd felt awkward, and though he shouldn't have responded at all, he decided to say something short and funny to defuse a bomb. Instead, he set it off. He kept his job, but the pain and emotional energy it cost him and his family will be felt for years.

As Jesus followers, we need to be especially careful of what we say online not only because we represent Jesus but also because what we say has the potential to be read by many and to affect people's opinions of us and of our churches. Our effectiveness as ministers of the gospel can be severely hampered by saying stupid things on-line. Many times, this can be remedied with a little self-disclosure and admittance of wrong, but gossip online has the potential to echo through eternity. And in some cases, it can cost us more than lost respect.

The Fidelity Question

Steve had a good marriage. Sure, he and his wife had the normal marital issues but nothing outside of what every other ministry couple encounters—money; raising children; ministry stress.

At first, the other woman was just a Social Networking friend. However, the information he posted about what he was doing and where he was going made it easy for her to show up in the same places. Steve started to notice this, but he didn't fight it. He flirted with her. "It was great to see you today at the coffee shop!" "How do we keep ending up in the same places? LOL." This turned into an online affair with a woman who liked what he had to offer the world. Steve ended up offering her himself.

One day, this woman sent an Internet message intended only for Steve, but she made a mistake in the sending process. The message went across the globe. Steve is now getting a divorce.

Not too long ago, Jenny got into Social Networking to tell people about her new job and hopefully find some new clients. In the process of adding friends, she added her old high school boyfriend. Her husband saw that she had added him and protested, but she assured him that everything was okay and that the old boyfriend was happily married and living in another state far away. Jenny's husband let it slide but told her to be careful.

When Jenny planned a trip to New York for business, she posted it online. Her old boyfriend told her in a private message that he was going to be in New York as well and said they should meet for dinner. Against her better judgment, she agreed. She then kept the interaction a secret from her husband so he wouldn't be worried. She told herself there was no danger. Dinner led to conversation; conversation led to lunch the next day. Lunch led to another dinner. Dinner led to a sexual encounter that "wasn't planned and took her by surprise."

Risky and Risqué

Online risks exist for adults as well as for children. However, most of the trouble adults find themselves in has nothing to do with predators or spies or friends with poor judgment. Adults are good at baiting their own hooks. The risks for adults online are greater and have more devastating outcomes than the risks for children. The risks for our children are greatly reduced or eliminated by parental involvement, safety controls, monitoring, following legal guidelines, observing site age restrictions, and common area computer usage.

However, there are some online risks that can only be eliminated by being proactive and creating accountability and editability. There are pornography filters and safe settings available for our computers, but the real dangers that exist are the ones for which there is no software filter. They are the risks that don't look risky at all—at first. They are the risks that exist right out in the open at times. They are the risks that exist when crossing boundaries that everyone crosses online every day without repercussion. They are risks that aren't inherently evil but still provide a gateway for failure.

Adults who should know better create their own vulnerability every day. If you are following all the laws and guidelines for safety, the chances that an online predator will abduct your child are slim to none. However, adults make choices online every day that result in the loss of jobs, families, ministry positions, money, and respect.

The book of James warns about being dragged away and enticed by our own evil desires. James pictures us as fishers who dangle temptation in front of our own eyes and flirt with it. We bait the hook. We throw it in the water. We bounce it around in the stream. And it looks so good to us that we eventually bite it—forgetting about or ignoring the danger. In the past five years I have witnessed bad things happen, including divorces, because of romances that began online.

In the past few months, I have counseled multiple couples whose marriages are in turmoil or ending because of relationships fostered between a spouse and an "old friend" on a Social Networking site. Every one of them began "innocently." Two began when the people were starting conversations about Jesus.

We need safeguards in place in every communication venue. Safeguarding comes with conversation, prayer, accountability, question asking, and *never* allowing anyone to think he or she is beyond making bad choices.

Guidelines for Communication with the Opposite Sex

Online communication has the inherent risk of making us feel closer to people than we actually are. A Facebook post, an e-mail, a Twitter, or a Google+ conversation can make us feel like we have spent time with people. Reading people's updates and posts can make us feel like we know them.

Picture this scenario: one spouse goes to work in an environment where he or she is not allowed to use Social Networking at all. The other spouse works at a church that encourages it. The couple has a fight and leaves for work without resolving the issue. The disconnected spouse lives with tension all day without the ability to talk to anyone about his or her pain. The connected spouse updates his or her profile with, "I wish I could take back some things I said." A cyberfriend of the opposite sex sees the post and responds, "How can I pray for you?" The connected spouse replies, "Don't worry. Just had a fight this morning." The cyberfriend replies, "Sorry. Remember that everyone makes mistakes."

See what is happening here? The connected spouse goes home having had a conversation with someone of the opposite sex who gave him or her encouragement and understanding. The disconnected spouse had no such conversation, still feels hurt, and had no idea the interaction took place. Don't fool yourself into thinking these interactions don't seed potential for devastating effects.

Before Social Networking, some details about people's lives were reserved for face-to-face conversation over a long period of time. However, a quick glance at an online profile has the potential to make us feel more intimate with a person than we actually are. It isn't something we need to fear; it is something we need to be aware of and take precautions for. Objects in the Facebook mirror aren't as close as they appear.

In some ways, profile snapshots are very helpful. For instance, I like knowing when people on my ministry teams are undergoing family pressure, work complications, financial problems, and spiritual crises. This information helps our teams communicate well and minister to one another.

The danger lies in the use of that information to manipulate people. For instance, it's easy for a person who is going through a relationship struggle to feel attracted to a person who posts pictures of his or her family having a good time together or who mentions how lucky he or she is to have a spouse like the one he or she has. We don't have to feel like a predator or a manipulator. Human nature fills in the gaps for us to make it a reality if we are not careful.

We should always be cautious of physical touch with the opposite sex. However, with the perceived instant intimacy Social Networking provides, we should be all the more careful. The fist bump and the side hug are your friends. Beware the full-on frontal hugs. Hugs aren't evil. Jesus likes hugs. Most men like them too—a lot.

Be careful not to establish ongoing counseling relationships with anyone in a one-on-one scenario. Encourage meeting in threes or even fours. Extended online one-on-one communication can be extremely dangerous. Because the dangers aren't present like they are in face-to-face meetings, "meeting" online sounds nonthreatening and gives the false sense that everything is aboveboard.

Ask yourself, "If my spouse or coworkers knew this conversation was happening, would I have it?" Or "If I conversed with this person face-to-face as often as we do online, would there be suspicion or danger?" Chances are the risks are the same, if not intensified. Make no mistake; private online conversations are just as dangerous as a secret rendezvous—perhaps even more so. We will say things online that we wouldn't say in person. It feels less risky online so we take the step.

Be careful of direct messages and "secret" messages. Whereas Social Networking can enhance ministry connections and effectiveness, it also carries a high degree of potential danger for relationships to bloom into something unhealthy. Whenever you engage in online conversation that is not public (a direct Tweet; an e-mail; a Facebook message), you should keep it short. It doesn't hurt to make someone aware of the transaction.

Whenever I get an e-mail or message from a female online, I let my wife know. It's not necessary to sound an alarm for e-mails that are short encouragements or simply full of information about an event. However, beware of ongoing e-mails that are more personal in nature. A "good job this weekend" e-mail is okay in and of itself, but if it comes every week, be cautious.

When communicating online with the opposite sex regarding a serious, relational, or potentially volatile situation, consider having a staff member or your spouse proofread the message. As a policy, operate with full disclosure. At any time, an accountable staff member should be able to read what you have written to anyone in an e-mail, Facebook message, Twitter, and so on, unless it is a private family matter. Be careful of your wording.

Do you only friend the pretty people? Do you seek out your attractive acquaintances online? My personal rule about adding friends on Facebook is that I don't seek out female friends unless they are family or very close friends. In the case of very close friends, I make my wife aware of the addition and even suggest that my wife become friends with that person as well. In most cases, I ask my wife permission before initiating the request of a female friend. The only exception to this is when I am adding multiple ministry team members. In any case, my wife has full access to my Social Networking platforms, including my passwords.

With a trusted staff member or close friend whom you've invited to edit you, be willing to fess up to any online crushes and infatuations. These things happen and should be dealt with. Confess and ask for accountability.

Learn to communicate love and appreciation for someone in ways that include the couple or the whole group. For instance, constantly telling someone of the opposite sex that you love and appreciate him or her is not bad per se, but it isn't wise. "We all love you and appreciate you" is much safer. Consider thanking someone's spouse at the same time you thank him or her: "Dear Madam X, thank you so much for the time you spent cleaning the classrooms. We love your dedication! Please thank your husband, the guy who doesn't know I sent this letter, for holding down the fort at home while you served here. You are both heroes!" Or "Here is a gift card for you. I hope you and your wife enjoy a great night out on the town!" which sounds much better than, "Go buy yourself something nice. You deserve it!"

Practice full accountability disclosure when working on long-term projects with the opposite sex. Oftentimes, when we are involved in projects together, online communication is necessary. However, projects have the ability to stir unhealthy feelings toward each other. It is possible to enter a project completely innocently and serve in the name of Jesus and come out on the other side with an unhealthy attraction. This is also true of crisis situations.

Be careful of online counseling with those in broken relationships. Your compassionate ear and love will be foreign to them, and feelings for you may develop. This will affirm you and probably make you think more highly of yourself than you should.

Andrew and his wife sat in my office to ask advice about Social Networking. Andrew's wife did not want him to have a Facebook account because he had once had an affair. Andrew's response was, "She doesn't trust me, and it's ruining our relationship." Andrew was only partly right. She didn't trust him. However, their relationship was not becoming ruined because of her lack of trust, but because he had had an affair. Furthermore, when his wife expressed her fears about his online relationships, he only furthered her suspicions by his insistence that he should have the right to talk to whomever he wanted to online.

I suggested two possible scenarios for Andrew and his wife. The first scenario included Andrew giving his wife all his passwords, full access to his Social Networking, and the privilege of raising concerns over friends or conversations. In this scenario, his wife would agree to listen to his reasons for being friends with females, but she would have ultimate veto power. In the second scenario, Andrew would cancel all his Social Networking accounts.

None of us needs Social Networking to survive. Although the premise of this book is about the benefits of Social Networking for ministry, there are exceptions. For some, it is wise not to foster unmonitored relationships with the opposite sex at all. Andrew is a perfect case in point. He doesn't need it for work. He doesn't use it for ministry purposes. Even if he did, based on his past he should be open to his wife monitoring his online behavior.

Andrew was furious with his options. He replied, "Her lack of trust is driving me away." "No, Andrew," I replied. "You are driving a wedge by not letting your spouse into your world. The guidelines help build the very trust you desire. Your reaction suggests you have something to hide even if you don't—yet." When we damage marital trust, online communication is no longer the "right" we thought we once possessed.

The Space Between and Things Left Unsaid

Another potential danger in online communication is not the words we say but rather the words we don't say. Our posts and updates have the potential to bait further investigation and raise a series of questions. Sometimes this can be fun. Other times it can be dangerous.

One of the stupidest moves I ever saw a pastor make occurred when I was in Bible college in Portland. You be the judge, though I already gave you my opinion. The pastor in question stood in front of the congregation on a Sunday like any other. The church was doing a series on biblical sexuality. This Sunday the sermon was on temptation. Pastor X delivered a great sermon but ended with a statement that went something like this: "Everyone is tempted. Even pastors face temptation. No one is above it. I admit, I am tempted too. There are even ladies in this very congregation who I am tempted by."

Immediately ladies began to wonder, *Is it me?* His wife began to wonder, *Who are they?* His staff began to wonder, *Are they married, young, old…?* Sometimes what we don't say invites trouble. The pastor got fired because of what he had called "self-disclosure" in preaching. Others called it weird and creepy.

Pastor X did a bit of baiting that fateful day. He might not have known it, but in all honesty, I think he did. So did his staff. So did the ladies of the church. So did his wife. At times our baiting conversation and questions are actually more like advertising. The space between our words becomes that much more dangerous when it creates potential for relational conflict. The way we word our updates has the potential to stir investigation. "Enquiring minds want to know."

Diane was going through a divorce. No one knew it until she posted online, "Is there such thing as a man who understands?"

Rosie once posted, "Sometimes men are jackasses."

Joseph posted, "Win some. Lose some. Adios."

What are the immediate questions that come to your mind? Do you think these people knew what they were doing? Do they understand the power in words left unsaid? Of course they do. All of these posts immediately had follow-up comments. "Are you okay?" "What's going on?" "Don't tell me it's over!"

Sometimes we bait conversation and questions not just by one single post but also by a string of posts or consecutive themes in our updates. Jeff was frustrated by his job at the church. He was thinking about leaving and going elsewhere. He started an online search for a job. Soon he was posting things like, "Wow! Did you know Church XYZ had such an awesome art focus?" And "Talked to a friend in Houston today. We can learn a lot from churches like his." And

"Just read the new book by Pastor Z. I like this thinking!" It didn't take too many more of these posts for his senior pastor to call him in and ask if he was happy.

Posts that bait further conversation, interaction, and raise questions are manipulative. In some cases, the manipulation is all in fun and the audience is aware of it and approves of it. In some cases, the manipulation leads down a destructive path.

Kyle had a string of posts that went something like this: "Dinner for one tonight. Homemade pasta!" "House is empty. Time to watch a shoot 'em up movie!" And "Silence is okay sometimes. Other times it's loud." Kyle had quite a few friends ask why he was alone, where his wife was, and if everything was okay. His posts caught the eye of one woman in his church who was going through a tough time. She sent him a note asking if he wanted to talk.

Soon, Kyle and the other woman were sharing their struggles and crying on each other's shoulders. The sharing online led to coffee shop meetings. Those led to the bedroom. All this flirtation that led to their sexual escapades was first fostered in an environment of things not said.

The Heart of the Matter

Sean was a fellow pastor friend of mine. He thought these cautions were ridiculous. He once turned these cautions against me and told me I might think more highly of my own attraction potential than I should. He said, "I'm not going to walk around feeling paranoid or in some delusional state that every woman wants to be with me." Although I understand Sean's perspective, these cautions have nothing to do with what I think about my own attractiveness. They have more to do with creating an environment for attraction to grow between any individuals, regardless of how initially desirable they may be.

If your relationships are worth protecting, you will be willing to take steps and precautions. Create guidelines such as those outlined in this chapter. Sit with your spouse, your coworkers, and your friends. Talk through the dos and don'ts. Put together an agreement. Big mistakes begin with tiny surrenders and small decisions.

Conclusion

There was a joke when I was in college that illustrated the church's common response to the presence of danger. "Why is the church opposed to premarital sex? Because it may lead to dancing." Social Networking is a dance. There is nothing inherently wrong with it. In many ways it is beautiful. It is a perfect place to invite people to join in the celebration. Just because one hurting soul hikes up her skirt on the dance floor or someone calls his date a name, there is no reason to panic and cause a stampede. The building is not on fire. Don't ignore those people and don't abandon the dance.

As Jesus followers, we are called to be influencers. Truth tellers. Encouragers. Teachers. Empathizers. And we are called to give people the tools they need to navigate in an unstable and volatile world. It is instinctual for us to avoid danger. The church for far too long has abandoned, restricted, or bad-mouthed art, culture, and technology when danger is present. We don't do anyone any favors or gain any ground by ignoring threats around us. We can only truly protect, inform, and help people navigate the risks when we understand the mediums. As one blogger recently wrote about the risks of Social Networking, "Knowledge is a fantastic repellant of ignorance and disastrous behavior."

One of my favorite Plato quotations is, "Those who tell the stories rule society." As Jesus followers, we need to be proactive about telling the stories that matter. Our stories are the ones the world needs to hear. The more we tell them and the more venues we tell them in, the more commonplace those stories become. Our voices become louder. Our hopeful voices become the trusted news sources.

Post: What Would Jesus Tweet?

The Provincial Life

Disney's *Beauty and the Beast* is my favorite animated feature. Belle (one of two protagonists) lives in a world that is fast paced and reeks of meaninglessness and banality. However, it's not the asphalt ocean of Los Angeles and it's not 2012. Belle's world is a small French blue-collar village full of bakers, barbers, and booksellers in the 1700s.

The opening song, "Belle" (aka "Little Town"), is a dreamy sequence where Belle cries out, "There must be more to this provincial life," while passersby exchange common greetings, thoughts, quips, and—might I suggest—sound bites. "Bonjour!" "Good day." "How is your family?" "I need six eggs." "That's too expensive." Belle is polite but doesn't have much time for this fruitless conversation. She buries herself in books where she reads of adventures that live outside of her monotony.

This is often a critique of Social Networking—it's frivolous. It doesn't add anything to an already busy life. It's a waste of time.

I have three children. Two are college age. My youngest is in middle school. When she comes home from school, I ask her questions about her day. "Who did you hang out with?" "Was the lunch I made for you filling enough?" "Did anything exciting happen?"

Oftentimes she has a bunch of great stories. I love to hear about all the quirks the children in her class have. There's the boy who makes

86

robot sounds all day. There's the girl who turns everyone's name into a nickname. There's the boy who often says hilarious things that are inappropriate for the classroom but are funny nonetheless.

When she tells the stories, she just wants me to listen; to laugh; to share in the experience; maybe to add a story of my own here and there about when I was growing up. She doesn't want my commentary on every situation. She doesn't want me to turn every child's story into a deep conversation. Sure, there are teachable moments. However, I'm her dad; I'm not her therapist. She doesn't want textbook responses about how everything ties into the great metanarrative. She wants to know that she can talk to me about everything and anything and that it isn't always going to be a heavy lesson. If I broke into a Ward Cleaver speech every time she told me a story about a boy flicking a booger on someone or sassing the teacher, she would eventually stop talking.

I think, as ministry folk, we often fall into the trap of thinking that everything is a teachable moment or an invitation for spiritual commentary ("Godmentary?"). Although it's wise to look for teachable moments, it's also wise to remember to laugh and to understand that the little things—the little exchanges—are all part of life. We need to play together well—and small talk is necessary in playing.

I love that Belle is buried in a book in the movie's opening scene. She reminds me of many people I know—theologians, teachers, artists, pastors, and dreamers—who are always saying, "There must be something more." I understand this sentiment. I am one of these people. I think a lot of people in ministry are like this.

If we are going to have a theology of the depths and mysteries unknown, we need a simultaneous theology of play or we will go crazy. And we will grow increasingly inward. Community and relationship require surface and shallow as much as they require depth.

I counsel a lot of couples who don't enjoy each other anymore. They don't date. Sex is a chore, if it happens at all. They are consumed with lack of money and with raising children. Oftentimes I will listen to their stories and ask, "When did you stop playing?" "When did life become so serious for you?"

When young couples go through premarital counseling with me and we talk through budgets, I always tell them to budget fun money and not to cut it out. When times get tough, the fun money is always first to go. Everyone talks about putting recreation money back in the budget someday, but they seldom do. And their lives slowly become business.

Social Networking can be full of depth—links to blogs and to informative websites, apt quotations, scripture, and advice. But it's potential is only fully realized when we allow ourselves to play.

Beauty and the Beast commences with Belle wanting "more" from life. Soon thereafter, she becomes a prisoner in the castle of the beast. She is taken away from the monotony of her provincial life. While she is a prisoner singing dishes and flatware serve her a dinner in the castle. The tension eases as they merrily sing. They assure her that "no one's gloomy or complaining" and that they tell jokes and do tricks "all in perfect taste." Playfulness becomes important in a prison. Belle's quandary and process of discovering what matters in her life come to fruition when all the mundane is stripped away. When it is gone, she longs for casual conversation with friends and family.

In essence, Belle wants a life that's meaningful and worth something in the provincial life. She doesn't have time for trivial pursuits. However, Belle ultimately finds love and relationship there in the village. She learns to value the small things and not to take things for granted. She learns to see beauty in "shallow" conversation. And she learns to see her village and its people through a set of caring and empathetic lenses as she embraces their experience and stories.

In the World, Not Of It

I have two friends who are both passionate about Social Networking. Jeff is passionately against it. Dan sees it as his mission field.

Jeff likes to remind Christians that they are to be "in the world but not of it." He wears the slogan like a T-shirt. For Jeff, being "not of the world" means abstaining from and sometimes demonizing certain things he deems necessary to avoid. He would be happy living in a cabin in the woods away from all civilization as long as Christians made that cabin and the products used had no potential for funding anything he might deem unchristian. Jeff calls Social Networking "a joke" on good days and "an abomination" on others.

Dan looks at Twitter and Facebook like some view church signs and marquees. He believes his cleverly crafted words might one day catch the eye of someone who is not a follower of Jesus, and he or she will be cut to the core and will surrender to Jesus. He spends a great deal of time invested in cyberevangelism and is fond of the saying "If one person comes to Jesus, it's all worth it."

Dan, like Jeff, believes strongly in being in the world but not of it. For him, being "not of the world" means not wasting his time talking or thinking about things that are not, in his mind, directly related to Jesus. He is guided by a phrase he has hanging above his desk: "What Would Jesus Tweet?"

If Dan, Jeff, and I were all still boys playing together and we decided to start our own clubhouses, the members of Jeff's club would have no fun. The Christian members of Dan's club would have fun. The members of my club would wage BB gun wars with the other two and be condemned for either owning a BB gun in the first place or for not having the right gun.

On Twitter, my name is @shameonyoko. It's a Beatles reference that requires no explanation for fans and too much explanation for those who aren't. Through a series of 140 characters tweets, let's explore these dramatically different views of Social Networking.

> **@shameonyoko** The concept "in the world but not of it" is not prescriptive or something 2 strive for. It is descriptive of who we are #whatwouldjesustweet

I have a bit of angst and righteous anger from growing up in a sheltered and sanitized environment. I have scars as long and as deep as the fangs of Fundamentalism and as painful as a hyper-Calvinist whipping. I don't always trust my ability to be polite when it comes to addressing the ideas that some Christians have of what it means to be "in the world but not of it," and I don't know if politeness is something I should even strive for.

I've seen family turn their backs on Jesus because of a long list of rules and regulations and the feeling that they can never do anything right or have any fun that is not sanctioned or created by the church. I know people who won't even talk about Jesus because of the multiple presentations of the gospel that they have heard from people more concerned about sealing the deal and winning arguments than they are about individual hurts and the condition of someone's life. And I have a long list of friends who have left the church.

As such, I am almost as passionate at times about rescuing my fellow brothers and sisters from their set-apartness as I am about conversing with a culture that doesn't yet know Jesus because my disengaged brothers and sisters aren't helping the Kingdom. They exist there, but they don't live there. And they certainly aren't inviting anyone in.

John 15:18-21 is one passage Christians refer to when talking about being "in the world but not of it." Here, Jesus is talking about our identity with him and how that alignment may not always be a popular choice.

If the world hates you, know that it hated me first. If you belonged to the world, the world would love you as its own. However, I have chosen you out of the world, and you don't belong to the world. This is why the world hates you. Remember what I told you, "Servants aren't greater than their master." If the world harassed me, it will harass you too. If it kept my word, it will also keep yours. The world will do all these things to you on account of my name, because it doesn't know the one who sent me.

In John 17:13-21 Jesus uses similar language while praying.

Now I'm coming to you and I say these things while I'm in the world so that they can share completely in my joy. I gave your word to them and the world hated them, because they don't belong to this world, just as I don't belong to this world. I'm not asking that you take them out of this world but that you keep them safe from the evil one. They don't belong to this world, just as I don't belong to this world. Make them holy in the truth; your word is truth. As you sent me into the world, so I have sent them into the world. I made myself holy on their behalf so that they also would be made holy in the truth.

As Christians, we are not part of "the system." Jesus has given us a new name. Foremost, at the core of our identity, we are children of God. The concept of "in the world but not of it" is not prescriptive or something to strive for. It is descriptive of who we are.

There are plenty of scripture passages that warn us about snares, mind-sets, patterns, and temptations to be aware of. However, there are plenty of other passages that encourage us to be light in the world, share the hope of Jesus, and invite people into the Kingdom. These passages are neither.

The phrase "in the world but not of it" has become a mantra for conservatives regarding what we can and cannot be involved in as Christians. I have heard it used in the context of everything from music and movies to towns we can and cannot visit ("Nothing will ever have to stay in Vegas if we never visit it in the first place") to the Internet and more recently and specifically to Social Networking.

> **@shameonyoko** There are two strong clubs in regard
> to Social Networking: avoid it altogether or (re)claim it
> as your own and use it #whatwouldjesustweet

For others, the same mantra is spun differently. Their goal is to make things that are not "Christian," Christian. "Christian" has become a descriptive label for things, as if they were mint or cherry. "Christian" is the new "sugar-free."

Many of my brothers and sisters, like Jeff and Dan, choose one of two clubs when it comes to Social Networking. The first club wants nothing to do with it, believing it is the devil's playground where idle minds hook up with the person of their dreams who happens to be someone other than the person to whom they are married. The second club views Social Networking (as a fellow Twitterer recently put it) as a "Canaan for Christians to conquer." Both clubs are in danger of not being any good to anybody for the sake of the Kingdom.

The first club is reminiscent of one I know all too well. When I was a teenager, we went on an outing to the river, and the pastor hung blue tarps all around the perimeter of the camp so that the men of the church would not be tempted to look at bikini-clad women. We were taught to blow up the television and burn all our rock albums. Everything was secular versus sacred. I was not allowed to spend the night at "nonchristian" homes. The people of the church weren't concerned about who they were influencing, but rather who was *not* influencing them or their children. In this club of set-apartness, most things were pretty black and white.

The second club is like one I spent time in for a while by choice later in life. Here, the basic premise is: not all things are inherently bad for Christians; we just have to clean things up a bit, sanitize them, and redeem them. If you buy this premise, anything has the potential to become a useful tool in the hands of Christians. Some things might even be enjoyed if they have the right look, lyrical content, or objective, or if there is the perception that there's a godly motive behind them. And, most important, everything can and should be used as a means of evangelizing the world.

Two extreme clubs: avoid it altogether or (re)claim it as our own and use it.

Of course I have painted with large brush strokes. The clubs aren't quite this distinct all the time. Some are much more militant on the first club's end of the continuum, and there are varying degrees of the second club as well. However, although the strokes are broad, I believe there are warnings to heed, questions to ask, and dangers to be aware of in any club or at any end of the continuum.

> @shameonyoko Do we know how to talk anymore? How to have regular, even mundane conversation? Is everyone who's not a Xian a project? #whatwouldjesustweet

If you do a search for "Christian Social Networking" you will find a myriad of sites where Christians can enjoy the Social Networking experience but can make more certain that they are networking with other Christians. I won't list any of them here. Suffice it to say, these sites lean dangerously toward the first club of asceticism and set-apartness. They are void of relationship with anyone who is not a club member.

Those who see Social Networking as their mission field don't need alternative media, but they make darned sure everything they say in 140 characters or less is going to count for something. By that I mean there is no silly talk; no casual conversation; nothing frivolous. It is all Bible verses, C. S. Lewis quotations, and the Roman's Road to Salvation.

This stance on Social Networking leans to the second club's end of the continuum. They certainly are involved in Social Networking, but they speak only their own club dialect and leave little room for spiritual conversation and engagement with people who don't know the language unless someone on the outside decides to challenge or ask questions—or unless they are lucky enough to stumble upon a secret decoder ring.

However, the problems here in both of the above scenarios are much larger than mission drift or philosophical differences. The problem is larger than forgetting with whom we are supposed to be communicating. The problem is we are losing the ability to communicate, period. And it's our own fault.

Shifts in Communication

If I went back in time twenty or so years and had a conversation with my younger self, Younger Me would not have any clue what I was talking about if I used words like *Internet, Social Networking, Twitter, Facebook, hard drive, RAM, direct messages, instant messages, RSS feeds,* or a hundred other words I use on a daily basis— and I'm not even a computer geek.

Today, these words have not only infiltrated the world of those who are saturated in technology; new media influences the way we talk in every kind of venue. In early 2011, the *Oxford English Dictionary* added the acronyms *OMG* and *LOL* to its list of legitimate English expressions and words. The dictionary defines these acronyms as "initialisms," since the initials together represent a common phrase.

This new communication shift is different from terms and phrases taking on new meaning over time. The shift is different from *cool, boss, cherry, hot,* and *hickey* meaning completely different things from 1952 to 2012. The current language shift is an introduction of new words, phrases, and expressions that are being created in one medium and hemorrhaging into the next. It is more akin to what would happen if everyone started talking in military language or using medical doctor terms in everyday language.

In some ways, many are being forced to learn the new language because of technology saturation in the home and workplace. However, the church at large has a history of downplaying cultural shifts and even ignoring or ostracizing them in favor of another kind of Utopia where everyone "gets back to basics" and isn't bothered by the things of the world—a world where we "simply focus on Jesus."

My fear is that the church will continue to ignore new ways of conversing—sending and receiving messages—and will not be able to clearly communicate the timeless message of hope and abundant life that Jesus invites the world to be part of. It has happened. It is happening.

Or we will not completely ignore the new ways of conversing; we just won't converse in participatory, helpful, constructive, and inclusive ways. We'll continue to talk the way we talk but within a new medium, with our own dialects, creating safe alternatives within those mediums or using the new mediums as our bullhorn.

When I was young I always loved hearing my grandmother's stories about growing up without a private phone, a color television, a microwave, or any of the other technology I took for granted as a child. In her day, new technology that revolutionized the world or changed the way the family operated came around every few decades.

Now, new communication technologies are not only delineating between grandchildren and grandparents; new technologies are delineating siblings in the same house. It is possible that children in the same household can be broken up between pre- and post-Internet and pre– and post–Social Networking.

Learning to communicate with one another is no longer relegated to tone, verbal and nonverbal expressions, and proximity. New communication technologies like Social Networking are requiring us to become multilingual in order to seek to understand one another in our own homes, let alone the world that surrounds us.

It's been said that effective communication is based on a person being able to understand the context and the symbols associated with the culture. That context and those symbols are being created and re-created daily in the world of Social Networking. Avoiding, ignoring, or trying to mask them does no one any good.

Wherever you place yourself concerning any club or varying degree thereof, there are some things in scripture that cannot be ignored:

Jesus never said, "Be in the world and hide from it."

He never said, "Be in the world and ignore it."

He never said, "Be in the world and create a new one kind of like it but much more sanitized."

He never said, "Create a Christian world," as if "Christian" were an adjective we could attach to things.

Yet that's what many have created all over the continuum of cultural involvement—the "other world." The Christian other world has its own products, marketing system, and language. Often the products are copies and sanitized remakes of the original idea that came from somewhere "not Christian." And it has at its core two guiding principles: a safe alternative for Christians and an evangelistic campaign.

It all starts so innocently—alternative media we can trust for our children; spreading good cheer; positive messages. But if we aren't careful, we begin to lose connection with the world around us. We live safe within our walls while the world goes through hell, and even our best and boldest evangelistic endeavors go unnoticed or ignored because the world doesn't speak our language and we don't know the world's.

@shameonyoko If something is damaging 2 the Kingdom, we may find remnants of hope within its fallout but it doesn't make it worth it #whatwouldjesustweet

I assume we agree that completely ignoring the world is not a good idea. Most people reading this book probably take issue with my first friend, Jeff. You probably wouldn't have picked up a book on Social Networking in the first place if you were in Jeff's club. You would look at this book as kindling.

However, you might agree or empathize with my other friend, Dan, on some level. You might feel somewhat of an evangelical burden to converse in Social Networking platforms while making sure every word counts; minding your manners; using apt quotations and recommending the right books.

You shouldn't feel bad for this core desire. I don't take issue with the desire to use Social Networking as a tool for communicating the gospel. Rather, as my wife has told me on a number of occasions (rightly so), "It's not what you say; it's how you say it" that becomes the issue.

Asking the question "What Would Jesus Tweet?" is not necessarily bad or misguiding, but it has the potential to go awry depending on how we think Jesus might say something and if we think Jesus would say it in that way to the whole world.

In Belle's provincial life, she is very kind to the baker, the barber, and the bookseller. They are all townsfolk who have added Belle as a friend in their network. They experience life with her. In the monotony of the provincial life, Belle never has to wonder if they love her. They ask questions and show genuine interest in her.

There is one person who very quickly becomes obviously annoying to both Belle and us, the viewers. His name is Gaston. Gaston has his eye on Belle. He is consumed with himself and sees Belle as a prize to be won. She tries to be kind to him, but he belittles her for reading books with no pictures and tells her there are more important things to think about—like him. He tells her that the whole town is talking about her and her frivolous activity, adding, "It's not right for a woman to read. Soon she starts getting ideas and thinking." His idea of a good time is showing her his hunting trophies and mocking the things and people she loves.

As onlookers, it is easy for us not to like Gaston. He is annoying and shallow. But Gaston doesn't see it. If he had the ability to listen to wisdom, we would tell him that is not how love works. His approach is all wrong. If he ever wants a chance with Belle, he has to have and demonstrate genuine interest in her, in the things she is interested in, in her family, in her dreams, and in the things that keep her awake at night, her fears and her longings.

Gaston reminds me of another townsperson that Disney didn't introduce. But he is in a lot of towns, and you would recognize him. He's the street preacher who stands on the street corner yelling, "Turn or burn!" Everyone is a project to this guy. Everyone is someone to be won over.

The street preacher comes in different flavors. Sometimes he wears an angry sign that says, "God hates fags." Sometimes he stands outside a concert and pickets it because the artist has questionable lyrics.

But the street preacher isn't always militant. Sometimes he passes out tracts on the corner and starts conversations with a question about hell and if a person thinks he or she might end up there.

When I see this guy I sometimes see hurt, a message based on fear, and a person void of relationship skills. No one ever sees this guy and thinks, *Finally, someone cares about me.*

I never want to be this guy. I never want to be Gaston either.

People certainly don't become followers of Christ by being beat up with scripture. And I would argue that they don't become Christ followers because of cleverly crafted propositions and pithy grabbers on bumper stickers, church signs, T-shirts, YouTube, Twitter, Facebook, LinkedIn, or any other media.

Some people might argue that point. Some might even have a story to tell about how someone surrendered to Jesus because of a slogan or a quotation. Some might take Dan's position: "If one person comes to Jesus, it's all worth it." But the stories would be infinitesimal, and Dan is wrong. If something is damaging to the Kingdom, we may find remnants of grace and hope within the fallout, but it certainly does not make it "worth it."

Does the offer of a life with Jesus get lost in the static of the other offers that come at us continually in the cyberworld? Is it possible that sound-bite evangelism sounds no more appealing than any other offer that guarantees happiness in cyberland?

As soon as someone opens an e-mail account, it seems as if a tiny troll peeks through the window of that person's home and begins e-mailing her or him offers of a better sex life, videos of housewives who are home all alone and wanting company, offers to purchase stocks, and letters from princes who deposited large sums of money into an account just for that person.

Somewhere, in the middle of all this, someone is tweeting the four spiritual laws. And my friends who don't know Jesus don't care.

> **@shameonyoko** It's wise to examine pitfalls of potentially off-putting techniques 4 communicating the gospel thru the lens of history #whatwouldjesustweet

Sound-bite evangelism is most often viewed as something "those crazy Christians do," even if this is not the case or the motive. And at times, it's simply chuckled at because of its tendency to come across as insincere, trite, or religious gobbledygook.

With all this said, let me be perfectly clear: I believe God can use anything he wants to get someone's attention. I believe God sometimes reveals himself outside of relationship between people, even though I said earlier "relationship is paramount" in evangelism. I believe scripture—the Bible—is sufficient revelation of Jesus in and of itself.

I am not making a case for evangelism only being effective within relationship. I don't believe we have to be friends with someone to communicate the truth of the gospel message. But I also believe this is the exception in God's economy. He most often uses people to communicate the gospel. The church—his bride—is his Plan A to heal the world.

Social Networking has great potential for instruction, spiritual conversation, and, yes, even evangelism. But it is wise for us to examine the pitfalls of potentially off-putting techniques for communicating the gospel through the lens of history as well as entertain some possibilities of how we can be more effective.

Asking the question "What Would Jesus Tweet?" is not necessarily bad or misguiding, but it's limiting. We must exercise care when preaching in sound bites—care not to belittle people; care not to start fights; care not to sound abrasive; care not to sound like we are selling the ShamWow! gospel.

Sharing the Gospel in Social Networking

Here are some ways to share the gospel in Social Networking platforms while avoiding the pitfalls.

> **@shameonyoko** If u want people to be attracted to Jesus in you, update like a real person. Don't be the online version of yourself #whatwouldjesustweet

We did a message series on relationships recently at our church, and I told a few stories about my wife. I have her permission, especially if I am sharing all the good stuff. On that note, here is something

I appreciate about my wife: she doesn't care if the neighbor hears someone yell in our home or sees our children get out of line. She doesn't care if you know she isn't perfect.

My wife is a Pampered Chef queen. She has consultants all over the United States and has been working the business for nearly twenty years. Her consultants often come to her for advice on how to discipline children, where to find a good church, and how to raise a husband. She has shared her imperfect life with them, and Jesus shines through.

She almost prides herself in wearing the "real person" tag. Religiosity is a lie to her. She has nothing to prove. It's Jesus who does the proving. She loves Jesus. But she doesn't want you to see a perfect Jesus follower. She wants you to see a regular soccer mom who unwinds with a glass of wine and a good book, who lays her head on the pillow at night praying for strength to wake up and invest in people again.

People are attracted to my wife and her love for Jesus because she is real, genuine. You get what you get. People want to be like my wife—not because she's pretty, though she's smoking hot; not because her house is in order, though it's pretty spotless; not because she's got her life in order, though she is organized to an almost sickening degree. It's because she is legitimate. She is the real deal. She doesn't think she is better than you. And that's attractive.

When my wife shares online updates about herself, she talks about the food she eats, the books she reads, the places she goes, the things our children say, funny things she heard at church, ways she is investing in the community, movies she's watching, the concerts she goes to, and things that she and her friends are experiencing.

Many times, the only version of a person we see is the online version of that person—sanitized; never having fun; only talking about overtly "spiritual" things. This is one of the reasons people say online conversations are so impersonal. When you are not talking like a person, they sometimes are.

The following people are some of my favorite Christians to follow on Twitter. I know many people who aren't Jesus followers who love following them as well. I think it has something to do with their realness. @JamieTheVWM (Jamie Wright: The Very Worst Missionary), @GuerillaHost (David McDonald), @lensweet (Leonard Sweet), @itsauelgood (Amy Auel), @marklee3d (Mark Lee), @chrisfromcanada (Chris Vacher), and @jesusneedsnewpr (Matthew Paul Turner), to name a few.

Remember Belle in the marketplace—casual conversation; brief updates; laughter; watching her love her father; seeing how she handled Gaston. Belle was consistently Belle, and this made her attractive.

> **@shameonyoko** When updating online, invite people into conversation. Ask questions. Interact. Be interested, not just interesting. #whatwouldjesustweet

Some of the greatest and most underestimated tools in Social Networking are the ability to "re-tweet" on Twitter, "Like" something on Facebook, or simply repost something in any Social Networking venue.

The re-tweet is Twitter's "amen" button. When someone says something funny, poignant, thought-provoking, memorable, quotable, or that gives helpful insight, one can choose to re-tweet what he or she just said and in effect say "I agree" or "That was helpful" or "I hear what you're saying" to that person's network, which may or may not include people from the original tweeter's network. So, if you say something I think is worth repeating, I can re-tweet your tweet to my network, thereby drawing attention to you within my network.

This is powerful because it is validating and it initiates conversation. If you re-tweet me, it lets me know that you heard what I said. You may be inviting further conversation. You may just be giving me a nod. Either way, I know I'm heard and I know you're listening.

Sometimes, people in my church will re-tweet something I've said, and I take it as an invitation for further conversation. Many times, the people who re-tweeted me are begging for interaction and don't know how to engage me as their pastor. Maybe they are shy. Maybe they are embarrassed. Maybe they don't know what to say.

I often follow their re-tweet with a direct message that goes just to them to see if they want to talk. Below is a typical five-minute conversation/interaction between an imaginary person and me. (Note: "RT" means "re-tweet" and "D" means "direct"—only the sender and the receiver see the message when this command is given. If a double forward slash is used in a tweet [like this: //] it means someone is adding something to the original tweet. It's really easier than it sounds.)

shameonyoko John Voelz
I had a great talk with my daughter today when we went out for a daddy-daughter breakfast. Watching her grow is a happy sadness.

WWDude Church Guy
RT @shameonyoko I had a great talk with my daughter today when we went out for a daddy-daughter breakfast. Watching her grow is a happy sadness.

shameonyoko John Voelz
D WWDude Thanks for the re-tweet. Do you have children?

WWDude Church Guy
D shameonyoko Yes. My oldest is giving me a little trouble right now. Wish we could go to breakfast. That will be the day. Sad.

shameonyoko John Voelz
D WWDude Sorry, man. Are you in a satellite small group at church? Do you have anyone to talk to about this?

WWDude Church Guy
D shameonyoko No. But I've been thinking about it. Do you know of a good one?

shameonyoko John Voelz

D WWDude There are a few. I will tell Becky we talked today. She's in charge of satellites. Do you have her Twitter I.D.?

WWDude Church Guy

D shameonyoko No.

shameonyoko John Voelz

D WWDude You can reach her at @bcrumbs on Twitter. Let me know when you guys talk. I'll check back.

WWDude Church Guy

D shameonyoko Thanks, man. Looking forward. Loving Westwinds.

WWDude Church Guy

Had a great chat w/ @shameonyoko. Getting in touch w/ @bcrumbs 2 join a satellite group. I love my church.

shameonyoko John Voelz

RT @WWDude Had a great chat w/ @shameonyoko. Getting in touch w/ @bcrumbs 2 join a satellite group. I love my church.

//me 2, man. Thnx!

I also have conversations like this when people "Like" my status on Facebook by clicking the little thumbs-up button.

Asking questions is a powerful tool for inviting spiritual conversation in Social Networking as well. This brings up two good points: (1) Jesus was a question asker. He often answered questions with questions. (2) Jesus was interested in spiritual conversation. He didn't always try to seal the deal immediately with the person he was conversing with.

I think we would be wise to look at Social Networking as a conversation rather than a soapbox. This doesn't lessen your impact and influence in relationships. In fact, this is how relationships grow—through long-term investment and genuine interest in one another.

If you want to be successful with "evangelism" in Social Networking, you must be committed to the journey. Learn how to engage others and how to pull conversation out of people. Get to know them. Love them. And most important, be prepared to be there for them. Evangelism is not about speaking our minds and then being done.

Every once in a while, sometimes just for fun, sometimes looking for genuine feedback and answers, I throw a question out to my Social Networks. People love to share their opinions. In so doing, they stir conversation not only with me, but also with one another.

Some of the best Social Networking spiritual conversations I've had started with a question—and not necessarily an overtly spiritual question. "What movie do I need to see right now and why?" "What is the best fiction you've ever read and why?" "If your life was a song, what would it be?"

These are all questions that have questions behind them. They draw people into conversation about themselves. Asking about the "best fiction you've ever read" isn't just about a book. It's about what keeps people's attention, what interests them, what they want to know more about, and how they enjoy spending their time.

In this particular scenario, I received an answer back that the book *The Alchemist* by Paulo Coelho was a favorite. That book is about a boy's journey for riches and magic and power. Along the way he finds the meaning of life and love and relationship as well as his original items of interest. More important, he gains a new perspective. This is all rich fodder for communication, and it helps us as pastors and ministry leaders in shaping what happens on the weekend and throughout the week in the church life as we take the pulse of our particular culture and people.

Finally, keep this last important thing in mind when considering what evangelism looks like in Social Networking:

> @shameonyoko I can't be buddies w/everyone in my
> church. But Social Networking is a gift that allows me
> to be everyone's friend. #whatwouldjesustweet

People aren't commodities. Relationships are the core of ministry. We need one another. We know all these things if we are in ministry.

We also know it is impossible for a ministry leader to be friends with everyone, meet everyone's needs, and give everyone a listening ear. Not only is it not possible, it isn't biblical. God doesn't expect us to bear that impossible burden.

Scripture gives us much instruction about equipping the saints for the work of the ministry and understanding that we are a kingdom of priests. "It takes a village" is not an original idea. However, often-times in ministry we do feel the burden. We do want to help people. We do want to listen. We do want to give our time. This is natural, and at its core (without all the weird trappings of codependency and trying to fix people and needing to feel wanted and such), it is honor-able and applaudable.

Social Networking is a gift that has the potential to connect us to more people than we could possibly be connected to otherwise. They find us and friend us. We find them. We friend them. We friend their friends. They friend us. We are all in conversation together.

I had a man sheepishly approach me in the church lobby recently. "Thanks for being my friend," he said. I put two and two together and realized (since I never saw this man face-to-face before this time) that he meant on Facebook. "You're welcome," I said. "Tell me your name one more time." He smiled and gave me his name. He told me I had just accepted his friend request that week. "I've wanted to come talk to you after church before, but it's kind of scary to walk up to the stage." I told him I understood and was grateful that he had reached out. I asked him a series of questions about who he knew and how long he had been at Westwinds. I asked if he had visited our information booth and if he was interested in getting involved.

Through this lobby conversation, which began in the virtual lobby of Facebook, I set a follow-up appointment with this man to talk about some things he needed advice on. One Facebook befriending, one short lobby conversation, and one thirty-minute office appointment later, this man is now heavily involved at the church and feels a part of this community.

I'm not his buddy. I can't be. But I am his friend. And through our friendship, he has found a few buddies.

A couple of years ago, a young woman started following me on Twitter and sending occasional messages. She asked a lot about church. She didn't attend Westwinds, but a friend of a friend on Twitter told her I might have some advice to offer.

She told me she just watched my tweets for a while to see the way I talked. After following for a bit, she decided to engage in conversation. She was not a Christ follower at the time we started talking. She had a lot of questions about God and church. Religion was suspect. And then, the conversation turned magical.

She lived in New York, hundreds of miles from me. One day, she saw me tweet something about Portland, Oregon, a favorite city of mine and a place I would live any day of the week given the chance if I could just move Westwinds there.

Coincidentally (that's how she described it), she was in the process of moving to Portland and asked if I knew of any good churches there where people thought like we did and did ministry like Westwinds. Months later, she e-mailed me to tell me she was getting baptized at the church I had suggested and she had met a lot of great friends there.

Our meeting in the lobby of Twitter was not a coincidence. I believe God is using Social Networking in huge "evangelical" ways. And it's not so much *what* we say that matters. What matters is our willingness to engage and to listen.

Learn the world of Twitter with the supplemental guide *Tweet You Tweet Me: A Startup Guide for Churches,* available through Abingdon Press and ebook retailers. Go to www.abingdonpress .com/Voelz for more information.

The Church Lobby

As you may have figured out, I sneak out into the lobby between weekend services at the church. I have about ten minutes to shake hands and high-five there. Occasionally, I'll sneak off for a quick prayer with someone who grabs me.

The lobby (much like the provincial marketplace) isn't exactly a place to "go deep" with people, but it is certainly valuable. As I'm leading music or preaching, I look around the room and make eye contact. The people who I briefly touched or conversed with in the lobby are always the most attentive.

Some may argue that the church lobby is not real community, much like they argue that Social Networking isn't real. But this is not a simple debate. It is a question of expectations. If I go into the church lobby expecting to have something monumental and life-changing happen in a brief connection or short discourse, I will usually walk away sad.

It's the same problem some people have with reading and under-standing the Bible. The Bible is the word of God. It is also a book. It has the same rules as any other piece of literature. Poetic device, au-thor intent, and the original language shape it. It is full of a variety of genres. I have to understand what genre I am reading or I might get frustrated. If I take the Proverbs as promises, I will be disappointed. If I read the poetry sections looking for deep and specific systematic theology, I will not be happy. The genres are what they are.

Likewise, in the church lobby, if I expect the kind of community that sharpens, challenges, and edits me in my Christian journey, I have a wrong set of expectations. However, some form of community is taking place there. A smile, in and of itself, is meaningful. Sometimes a smile leads to something much bigger.

Social Networking is a virtual smile in the World Wide Lobby.

There's another thing I notice about the church lobby. I can always walk throughout it and find people who are new, bashful, frightened, and sometimes hoping to be noticed. Here, I get to extend my hand and introduce myself. It's not weird to meet one another in the lobby. It's expected.

Some of my most committed volunteers at Westwinds are people I met through the virtual lobby. At first it was hard for them to join a small group or show up to a function, but it was easy for them to start following me on Twitter or Facebook—hoping I would return the favor and we could get to know one another. That's part of the deal—meeting one another; starting conversation.

I had seen Jason and Erin at church before, but only from afar. One day we shook hands in the virtual lobby. Jason and Erin both started following me on Twitter. We had some casual conversation back and forth. Twitter broke the ice.

I quickly learned that Jason and Erin were hurting deeply. Erin had suffered a miscarriage, and they were looking for community to help them wade through the pain. A community of Twitter followers became their strength. Conversations in the virtual lobby started casually and turned into a great source of strength, camaraderie, and inspiration for them. To this day, Jason and Erin credit those early Twitter conversations for connecting them to a support network.

Three years later, one of my greatest joys is seeing the pictures Erin tweets of their healthy baby boy, Jonah; pictures of the crib Jason made; pictures of Jonah's first haircut. Occasionally, we catch a concert or dinner with Jason and Erin, and Social Networking keeps us in touch throughout the week. And it all started with a nod in the virtual lobby.

Just like in the church lobby, when we do Social Networking we engage in relationships. Healthy online relationships include a healthy understanding of space and a fair amount of self-awareness.

Cyberproxemics

My undergraduate work focused on communication, specifically public address. As a senior I taught speech labs for incoming freshmen. One of the most interesting topics in those labs was the science of proxemics. Proxemics is the study of space and the use of space.

Proxemics is important for an orator to understand. You wouldn't want to give a speech in a small room using large gestures and an overbearing voice. Likewise, you wouldn't want to be mousy in a large room where people have to strain to hear you or guess if you are still breathing.

When communicating, we are affected by physical space and by the distance between us and another human being. The type of space, the color, the decor, and what the space is usually used for affect us. The kinds of events held in these spaces also affect the rules of communication and our perceptions of one another.

There are many other factors that the study of proxemics concerns itself with, such as the physical cues we give one another, our nonverbal communication, our body heat, the environment, temperature, the way we touch one another, smell, and even the expectations we bring to each environment.

The study of proxemics has been very helpful to me as a pastor. Helping people understand what to expect in a given environment and educating our churches on how space works and affects us help us plan events, solve space issues, and teach about spiritual formation.

We communicate in different spaces—public, social, personal, and intimate. Loosely defined, think of public space as your church auditorium on a packed Sunday morning. Social space might be the newcomers' luncheon following the service. Personal space is the premarital counseling session you have with a new couple following the luncheon. Intimate space is when you go home and kiss your spouse, hold hands, and describe your long day. Each space has its own fair expectations. When we bring unfair expectations from one space into another, things go awry and get confusing.

Consider a woman who attends church once every other month, sits in the back corner, and then quietly and quickly slips away at the end of the service. One Sunday she approaches you, the leader, and says, "I'm leaving the church! There is no community here!" In many cases leaders get their feelings hurt, go overboard to make the person feel at ease, negate the person's feelings altogether, or employ a combination of any of those reactions. But is this response fair based on what we know about this person?

Her statement, "There is no community here," is based on unfair expectations of the space and her own lack of proactivity. She hasn't made herself known; she is rarely there; and most important, the space she occupies is not designed to necessarily foster the kind of community she is looking for. She has what is most likely a social space need and is trying to meet it in a public place.

Bryan hates every small group he has ever been a part of. Small groups don't meet his expectations. He had heard that a small group was the kind of place where he might get to know a close friend or foster a mentoring relationship with someone. But he hasn't found that kind of a friend in a small group. Every group he has been a part of has been full of people with whom he has nothing in common. So Bryan gave up on small groups, saying, "Those things are a joke." But are they? In reality, Bryan has unfair expectations of small groups for the kind of personal connection he is looking for.

Bryan never really invested in the kind of groups he was joining. He needed to be in what some might call an "affinity group" based on similar likes, ages, and part of town. Bryan is like many people who are told small groups are the cure for all their relational needs and sign up for one thinking it's their spiritual duty to join one. When they do, they are disappointed.

Proxemics and Social Networking: The Not-So Space

In some ways, Social Networking lives both in and between all four proxemic spaces. It doesn't fit nicely within any one of the spaces. At the same time, it is often utilized in most, if not all, of them, and messages are certainly received in all of them.

When I send a tweet to my wife, with whom I am as intimate as one can get with another person, the physical space from which I send it can alter my communication. If I am in a social space like the office at church, I might keep my words short and to the point. If I am in a social space like a concert, I might tweet a photo to show her the look on my face. The space I'm in affects the message I send regardless of the fact that my wife and I share an intimate relationship.

When my wife receives that message from me, she might be in the grocery store, which is a public space. Her reaction and response to my message will probably be different from the reaction and response she would have if she received that message while sitting at home. I might get my feelings hurt if she sends me back a message that reads, "Neat. Let's talk later," because I have expectations for the kinds of messages my wife sends me. I want her to be interested. But should I expect that of her while she is buying cleaning supplies?

From time to time, my daughter will send me a tweet while we are in the same house. Sometimes, just to be silly, she will send me a tweet from across the room that says, "I love you, Daddy." I have a level of intimacy with my daughter who is sitting with me in a social environment. The message is changed by the physical space of the room, my daughter's physicality, and what is happening in that room at that particular time.

Tweets from my daughter across the room communicate something different from tweets sent from school. There is a different kind of sentiment when we are in the same room and I am able to read her body language. I might read different things into her communication, such as playfulness or that special kind of flirting that little girls do with their daddies.

What happens in Social Networking affects all of the spaces we inhabit in life even if Social Networking isn't being used in the spaces we occupy at the time the message is sent. If I come home from the concert from which I sent my wife a picture and explain my frustration that she wasn't overjoyed by my message, and if I tell her this while we are standing in the bedroom, I have brought an argument into what is normally an intimate space. My reaction to my wife's lack of excitement reveals my ignorance of the space she was in when she received the message (not to mention that I might now have to sleep on the couch).

We need a new set of expectations for Social Networking that hasn't yet been defined. With a set of standards that are still being discovered, we need to gauge and filter the communication we initiate and the messages we receive. We need to be more cautious about our communication in Social Networking platforms because there are still so many questions.

What Space Is This?

It's Saturday. Rachael just invited David to her birthday party. Everyone is to meet in the school parking lot on Monday and take a bus to a comedy show. She sent the invitation out on Facebook. It was a group invitation. Everyone who received the invitation was able to see who else was invited to the party.

David has a crush on Rachael. He heard she might be having a party and hoped he would be invited. He's been picking up cues in different Social Networking platforms that she might like him as well.

Rachael does not have a crush on David. She thinks he's nice, but she only invited him because they are both part of the same university club, which has an online chat component. They have mutual online friends, and Rachael thought it wise to include him. In fact, they've barely talked in person. Most of their communication has been online.

David responds to the invitation with, "Heck yeah, I'll be there. Save me a seat on the bus!" Rachael immediately feels awkward. She wonders if David has a crush on her. He does, but that is not what he meant by "Save me a seat." Everyone else reads his response as well. Some read it as flirtatious. Others don't. Some don't care.

David and Rachael have something else in common—they go to the same church. On Sunday, they sit across the room from each other. Other party invitees are in the room as well. David, still feeling like Rachael has eyes for him, waves at her from across the room. He is sure she sees him. In fact, she doesn't see him and doesn't respond. He is crushed.

That night, on Facebook, David sends a message to Rachael in the same discussion stream where everyone who was invited to the party is privy to the conversation. "Is everything okay? You dissed me at church today."

Melissa reads his comment in the discussion stream and decides to send him a Twitter message. "@David. Hope everything gets patched up with Rachael." Melissa has a hundred followers. Most were not invited to the party, but many of them know David and Rachael.

Soon they all begin to ask questions. One of Melissa's followers is Rachael. She is embarrassed.

This scenario never would have happened before 2004. And as dramatic and convoluted as it seems, it is a pretty normal occurrence. When many of us were in our young teens, the scenario would have been much simpler. Rachael might have handed David an invitation. David would have had no idea who else was invited unless he had asked. David would have told her yes or perhaps called her on the phone to RSVP later that night.

In reality, Rachael probably never would have invited David before Social Networking. Their relationship is one that has been fostered and grown through online communication. Their online networks have influenced Rachael's loose affinity with David and her feelings of obligation to invite him.

David probably never would have had a crush on Rachael had it not been for Social Networking. His feelings toward her have been exaggerated by the sense that they have spent a lot of time together when in fact they have not. It is an illusion.

So what space was this relationship formed in? Where did the conversation take place? How did proxemics affect the outcome? David certainly thought the relationship was destined for something more intimate. Rachael invited David into conversation in a kind of social format. With hundreds of onlookers watching the interaction take place, it certainly seems like a public setting. The fact is this scenario was influenced by all of the spaces and none of the spaces at the same time.

It certainly felt right for Melissa to send David a message on Twitter. Facebook is public. Twitter is public. After all, the conversation was anything but personal since it was right out in the open on the World Wide Web. But Social Networks are not public spaces in the way we have known them in the past.

Social Networks don't give the benefit of physicality, facial expression, feel of the room, or reaction of the people as a group, to count as traditional public spaces. To mess with our minds even further, public spaces of the past would typically not allow for the kind of interaction this entire group had on Facebook in this scenario—all at once, with everyone having the ability to hear all the participants. The perceived public space of Facebook is actually much more personal since only a couple or a few are involved. Just like a packed church auditorium with a few people having a discussion in the middle of it, the space can be personal and public at the same time, but it's usually more one than the other.

This confusion about proxemics and online communication is why I like to refer to Social Networks as the "Not-so space." If you're confused at this point, you're in good company. Everyone is. David and Rachael certainly are. They don't know what hit them. It all got so complicated so fast. "Not-so" describes a space that is similar but isn't completely like the traditional space it resembles. It also sounds a lot like "Nutso," which is at times appropriate.

The Not-so space is quirky. Communication happens fast in the Not-so space. We aren't always aware of who is in the Not-so space with us. And while the Not-so space sure feels a lot like the traditional space that it may resemble at any given time, the communication results are often different.

Ministering in the Not-So Space

Shane's church decided to start a Facebook fan page for their church. He described it to his congregation as "another place where we can all talk about life and Jesus and our community—much like we do here at church."

Tracey misunderstood. She was new to Facebook. She thought her posts would go directly to the church pastors and staff, much like the questions she writes on the comment cards at church. Her first post on the church's fan page read, "I'm wondering if masturbation is okay for Christians. My friend told me I should stop because I am a Christian and I am married."

Janet saw an opportunity to use the page as a billboard for her personal groups. She posted pictures of aborted fetuses and political voting guides.

James was single and looking for love. He spent most of his time talking to females who posted on the page. Most were single.

Lorie posted her concern that most of the pastors of the church were not posting on the page, which from her perspective showed a general lack of interest in people and a lack of support.

Micah is a photographer who saw an opportunity to use the page to talk about his photos and to try to sell them.

Pastor Shane looked at the fan page after a week. He couldn't believe what he saw. He picked apart the list. Some of the posts angered him; some confused him; and some made him embarrassed for the person who posted.

Shane felt sorry for Tracey, who had revealed to the whole church her guilt about pleasuring herself. He was angry with Janet for posting the very things he told her not to display in the church lobby. He laughed a bit at James but was then instantly concerned for the females he had interacted with, thinking they might perceive James as creepy. He rolled his eyes at Lorie because she expected something of him that he never promised. He was a little peeved with Micah for taking advantage of the system.

None of these people had done anything out of line. None of them had done anything inappropriate in and of itself. However, most of the posts were awkward at best. None of these individuals had done anything outside the guidelines that Shane had set up for them. They all talked about "life" and "Jesus" and their "community," much like they did at church.

Tracey felt like she could come in to the personal space of the office on any day and ask a question as sensitive and as intimate as the one she had asked on Facebook. Janet often participated in the social and public spaces of pro-life rallies at the church. James was part of a singles group at church where he was social with other singles all the time. Lorie was being counseled at the church and would have felt free to express her opinions in that personal environment. Micah would have been allowed to post his business cards on the bulletin board in the public space of the church lobby.

Shane did not clearly define the rules of engagement or the expectations for the kind of interaction he hoped would happen on the site. He did not define the space. All of the posts were appropriate for the space the people thought they were in, and all of the people would have shared that same information in the traditional physical spaces at the church.

The onus is on Shane. Shane needed to clearly communicate the kinds of things he wanted to see and not see on the page. For Shane, it's too late to go back to the beginning, but he can certainly intervene and set up some boundaries.

Shane might consider offering classes at the church about Social Networking dos and don'ts and how the church sees people using the Facebook fan page. He might also consider being actively involved in the page he started, so he can intercept communication when it goes awry or does not fall within the guidelines. At a bare minimum, Shane can post the rules for the page on the page itself.

> Welcome to our fan page. Please remember everything you post here is seen by all the other fans. Please refrain from promoting or advertising anything personal or political. Our pastors don't monitor this page and only occasionally give input. This page is for you to talk with one another about spiritual things.

Shane should also consider being proactive and contacting the fans who wrote the more pertinent posts. He might have one of the female pastors in the office contact Tracey to talk about her concern. He might call Lorie and explain his involvement or lack thereof with the page. He might take James out for coffee and mentor him about trying to find a wife at church.

As Jesus followers, we have an opportunity to engage the Not-so space, steer wayward and inappropriate discussion, invite further discussion into more appropriate spaces, and help people steer through the lack of space perception.

If Social Networking is the church lobby, there are a lot of folk looking around at the signage and trying to find where to go. Look for them. They are the ones wandering about awkwardly. They are the ones who don't realize that they are speaking so loudly. Ask if you can help. If they have concerns that can't be immediately met, help steer them to the right source.

The lobby is high-traffic congestion and confusion. It is full of newcomers and founding members alike. Many of the new people in the lobby don't even know that they look awkward to the people who are there every week. Be a friend to them.

When you see James flirting with all kinds of girls in the lobby, invite him for coffee or lunch, or to your home for dinner. When you see the single mom with four children who is crying out for help, try to hook her up with other single moms who can offer support.

Finally, remember that while the lobby might not be an inappropriate spot for some kinds of communication, it may not be the best option. Try to determine the needs of people in the lobby so that you can direct them to the right space to talk and have their expectations met.

The Engagement Bell Curve

On one end of the bell-curve-shaped Social Networking continuum are cyberascetics who reject all technology. On the other end is a deadbeat father searching for old girlfriends on Facebook 24/7. In between are varying degrees of health and unhealthiness. Let's look at some missteps on the back end of the bell curve that we might title "consumption." Good use of the space of Social Networking requires a healthy self-awareness.

You're So Vain

Not too long ago a friend of mine tweeted, "Narcissus does not fall in love with his reflection because it is beautiful, but because it is his." If you need a Greek mythology refresher, Narcissus was a hunter who fell in love with his own reflection in a pool and died staring at it. This is where we get the word *narcissism*, which describes an "inordinate fascination with oneself."

My friend was only partly right. The story of Narcissus is one where he was indeed renowned for his beauty. But my friend was onto something very important. Beauty is in the eye of the beholder, and the only reason Narcissus knew he was beautiful was because people defined him as such over and over again. He believed it because people told him it was so and he told himself it was so.

Nemesis was the goddess of revenge and retribution. When someone succumbed to hubris or pride that was an offense to the gods, Nemesis stepped in. It was Nemesis who led Narcissus to the pool, knowing that his fascination with himself was a blind spot, a weak spot, a spot that Narcissus was not readily aware of. In Narcissus's case, it was his own pride that killed him—a pride that he was blind to or at least chose to dismiss. This is also the case with the rest of us.

Bob Dylan's "License to Kill" indirectly references Narcissus in a poetic and potent way: "Now he worships at an altar of a stagnant pool / And when he sees his reflection, he's fulfilled."

True narcissists put themselves and their loved ones at great risk. Studies show (and maybe you have experienced this yourself or witnessed it in loved ones) that narcissists have a greater tendency to become impatient, anxious, angry, depressed, lonely, and violent. Narcissists tend to suck the self-esteem out of those with whom they are in relationship. They plant a dose of despair and alienation in those they allow to be closest to them, often resulting in infidelity and terminated relationships.

Narcissists often create their own reality where they feel there are more eyes on them than there actually are. They spiral into depression when they feel they are unable to live up to what they believe are other people's expectations of them. Unable to live with their own failures, narcissists often self-destruct and fall prey to all kinds of addictions, including drugs, alcohol, and pornography.

Many times, narcissists will not take responsibility for their own actions, believing they are invincible, beyond reproach, that other people are at fault for making them the way they are, or all of the above.

Within every one of us lie the ingredients for the making of a narcissist. A dash of pride, a cup of unchecked spirit, a slice of a lack of accountability, and time on our hands are a great start. If we are not aware of the dangers, the world of Social Networking can be a perfect kitchen for putting these ingredients together. We shouldn't fear entering this kitchen. It's not the kitchen's fault when a meal is poisoned. But the ingredients exist in many a kitchen because we take them with us wherever we go.

We're All a Little Pubescent

I have a tween at home. Like most girls her age, she likes to take pictures of herself. She's finding out who she is, experimenting with her own style and flair. She's at an age where her physical appearance is unfortunately a large part of her identity.

She is the second little girl to grow up in our home. We've been through this before, and it doesn't get easier. As a dad, I often tell my girls they are beautiful the way they are, God made them special and unique, and not to let some boy tell them otherwise. I also tell them that every girl grows up to be a woman but not every girl grows up to be a lady. They need to protect the things that make them fine ladies.

In some ways, Social Networking makes everyone a tween. Even adults play dress up and give the world the best possible them they can think of in a one-dimensional cyberland. We stick out our chins and make our faces look longer while we pose for our own profile pictures. We worry about saying we "like" something online for fear people will think we are shallow or stupid. We worry about the time in between our tweets in case someone thinks our lives are uneventful.

Social Networking is often the place where we put our best foot forward—if it's our foot at all. We can be who we want to be, and we can be who the world wants us to be. We can put whatever version of us on display that we wish. We can (pretend to) hide our flaws.

Everybody wants to be liked at some level. We want approval. We want to be part of something special. And in the world of Social Networking it's easy to feel special. The very fact that some platforms provide a "Like" button illustrates this. It is also a way to feel deflated when we don't get the approval we expect.

What Is Your Ethos Like?

Ethos is an Aristotelian word used in the context of communication. If communicators have good ethos, we believe what they are saying because they are authentic. They are not snake-oil salesmen. They are smoking what they are selling.

Ethos has been ghettoized in our church contexts to mean vibe and flash and cool factor at worst and general feel at best. I was at a conference recently where someone asked me what the ethos of our church was like. I knew what he meant. He was asking if I thought he would think my church was hip and the kind of church he would want to attend. I had a hard time answering because he would have a better idea of my church's ethos than I do. I'm too steeped in my own church world to judge my ethos.

Whether referring to authenticity or cultural milieu, I cannot make good church ethos happen. The best thing I can do is influence our ethos by staying on mission, speaking the truth, picking music and service elements that seem truest to us, and allowing our own artists to create an atmosphere that flows out of who they are rather than creating an environment they once saw work somewhere else.

We can ruin our church's ethos by doing and saying things that don't feel right to our own personality; by incorporating elements that are packaged and fake to people; by slacking on our own creativity; by going through the motions; by pretending we are perfect.

We, like our churches, have an ethos. If our Social Networking ethos is favorable, it means there is at least a perceived authenticity on our part. The hard thing about judging cyberethos is that the words in print and the tiny avatar representing a person are only glimpses of that person—usually the best glimpses he or she has to offer or is able to concoct.

Like our churches, if we are concerned about ethos the best thing we can do is influence it. Make no mistake, bad ethos cannot be masked forever. Eventually people will find out the truth behind the avatar.

I once thought about becoming a college professor. I asked my college professor friend one day what he disliked about his profession. His number one complaint was that he had to "publish or perish." He explained that because he was at a respected university and was head of a department, there was a lot of pressure on him to publish in journals and to continue his education with the hope of wowing people (especially new college applicants) with new discoveries. The system put an incredible amount of pressure on him to be creative and to say something worthwhile.

The idea of publish or perish sounded horrible to me. Why would anyone want constant pressure to outdo the next person or to come up with the latest greatest idea? Why would anyone want the pressure of writing something in hopes that it would be published and republished and quoted and revered? Yuck. So, I eventually went into ministry.

Little did I know that the idea of publish or perish is one of the very things that often fuels ministry folk in Social Networking. My bad.

I met Lowell at a conference. He is a great guy and has a lot to offer his church. His church is very involved in its community. Lowell is creative. One day over lunch he told me he was discouraged. He had just started on Twitter and had shared a few of his ideas for ministry through some tweets but no one gave him any feedback. No one re-tweeted. No one replied with a thumbs-up click on the "Like" button.

Lowell told me he was feeling like a failure. To make things worse, he admitted that he was jealous of me. He told me he had seen some of the ideas we were incorporating at Westwinds and had tried them at his church, but they came off as corny. He said, "I wish I could pull off the kind of ethos you guys have created."

"Whoa! Hang on, Lowell." I asked him if the things they were doing in the community and the creative things they were trying on their own, without my help or hindrance, were working for them. He replied, "Yes. People seem to like what we do, and they say they are moving closer to God. It's just not at the level you guys pull off."

Lowell went on to tell me some of the ideas he put on Twitter. Honestly, I know why no one thought they were good ideas. They weren't. He was trying too hard to impress people. He was making himself out to be something he wasn't. He was tweeting about the things he thought people would want to hear. And he was missing the mark. *But* the mark he was missing was someone else's mark and a mark he wasn't called to hit.

Lowell had a Social Networking inferiority complex. He was like the person who approaches the guitarist at church and says, "You are so good. I only wish I could move hearts like you do, but I'm not a musician." This person fails to recognize the unique way God shaped her and how she indeed possesses wonderful gifts to move hearts. Who cares about guitar?

I encouraged Lowell to stop following (and in his case, cyberstalking) other pastors for a while. I suggested that he stop reading blogs and instead start telling the stories of redemption and creativity and victory that were coming out of his church. The results were amazing and surprising to Lowell. People "heard" Lowell's true voice and told him they were inspired by what was happening in his church. The people at his church felt valued and celebrated. His words were encouraging to the people with whom he was in real relationship.

Lowell learned something else through his new experiment. He wasn't really called to church ministry. He was trying to be something he wasn't. Now Lowell runs a thriving theater company in his town.

If you suffer from a Social Networking inferiority complex, the counteractive condition of your ethos is not because you aren't saying cool things but rather because you are not sharing things that are true to yourself. This ethos, or lack of it, speaks just as loud as its twin brother, the Social Networking superiority complex.

Pride Cometh Before the Fall

I sometimes like the sound of my own voice. I like to be thought of as clever, funny, witty, smart, and creative. Knowing this, I am highly allergic to self-promotion—most of the time. It's harder to recognize this in myself than it is to recognize it in others.

When people in the church gain a platform of some kind and make it a habit of promoting all the cool things they do, I find myself becoming suspect, bored, angry, and judgmental. Sometimes my own shortcomings and the things I see in myself exacerbate the abhorrence of self-promotion. I'm not always proud of the way I tease them. Then again, sometimes people need to shut up about themselves.

My friends and I have a term for pastors who have a particularly nasty habit of self-promotion. We call it "pastorbation." Giving it a name like this has helped us call out the beast and disarm it. When we see it happening we discuss it and ask ourselves how we are doing. Are we guilty too? Are we crossing lines?

In an effort to curb my lust for attention, I overcorrect the problem most of the time. If I feel like my voice is getting tiring or I have talked about myself too much, I withdraw and self-loathe. This over-correction is only another form of the same disease—Self-Identity Negligence disorder, or S.I.N. for short.

I have found that in light of my own identity issues, which range from self-infatuation to self-loathing, I need editors. My editors are the friends who keep me in line and remind me that at the core of my identity I am a child of God. I am not a self-made man, and conversely I am not a worm (contrary to the popular hymn lyric, though I'll give the writer room for poetic license). I am made in the image of God, and it is my responsibility and honor to glorify him.

It has taken me years of counsel, therapy, and the input of caring friends to come to grips with the fact that I have something to offer the world. I have a unique perspective. I have been afforded opportunities that have been great learning experiences, and I am a good storyteller.

I struggle over what people will think about me when I share my thoughts and ideas. Will they think I'm pastorbating? I can never quite answer this question for myself. I don't want to be accused of being distracted from the mission Jesus called me to because I saw my reflection in the Twitter pool.

And sometimes I am distracted.

So, I have surrounded myself with people who will keep me in check. They are my editors. I've invited them to amend me. My friend David is quick to say, "Lay off, buddy." My friend Dan is a great encourager and reassures me when I am doing well. He also warns me of things I might need to be careful of. My friend Michael has known me since fourth grade and can tell what is going on inside me even before I speak a word. He is a good sounding board.

My friend Len is a respected author and speaker. I respect him because he has handled his own fame very well. He has become a source of encouragement to me over the years. He will often point out the unique things I should share with others. He also tells me when I am being wimpy and selfish about sharing ideas for fear of what some might think.

Sometimes my editors are proud of me. Sometimes they carefully warn me. Sometimes they encourage me. Sometimes they lovingly scold me. Always, they are honest. They are not yes-men. They do not just tell me what I want to hear. This is a key component to keeping this particular distraction in line.

Caution: unless we are in relationship, it is dangerous and nearly impossible for you to judge my motives or for me to judge yours. Recognizing what looks like the self-promotion of others and being aware of warning signs are important, but we are never to do this publicly or without an established mutual trust. Rebuking someone we haven't been invited to edit is an ugly and hurtful thing.

As Christians, we need to be on the same battlefield. We all need editors. If a friend invites you to edit him or her, do so gently. While you're at it, ask someone you trust to take out a gentle red pen to your online presence as well.

If someone invites you to edit him or her, here is a list of sample questions you can ask. Or you may ask yourself these questions:

- Are you making a habit out of checking the number of followers you have?

- Are you depressed when those numbers drop or aren't steadily climbing?

- Are you making a habit out of checking your Social Media rankings?

- Are you re-tweeting people's ideas or only waiting for yours to be re-tweeted?

- Are you interacting with others online, posting on their walls, asking them questions, and showing interest in them as much as you talk about yourself?

- Are the things you are posting reflecting new ideas or how cool you are for thinking about them?

- How often are you updating your profile?

- If someone were to look at your profile, pictures, and updates, what would they say is most important to you?

- Do you justify the time you spend talking about yourself even when people warn you? Do you fight them?

- Do you compare yourself to more popular online presences and find yourself trying to outdo them?

- Do you brag to people about your online influence?

Michael has a blog, a Facebook account, a Twitter account, and about a hundred other Social Networking platforms with which he is signed up. In all fairness, part of Michael's job is to talk about the benefits of Social Networking and creating brands on the Internet. Michael has great advice and often shares it at moderately affordable conferences and seminars.

When Michael started in the world of Social Networking, he was a pastor at a healthy church. He had a wife and children, a dog and a cat, and he exercised regularly. Fast-forward five years. Today Michael lives alone. He feels empty and friendless most of the time—even though he has thousands of followers in his Social Networks. What happened in five years to cause Michael's demise?

Along the way, Michael ignored all the warnings his real friends gave him. They told him he spent too much time in his office on his computer. They told him he was starting to sound like he was full of himself. They told him to be careful because a lot of females were saying flattering things to him. Michael's wife was supersupportive of him, but she aired her concerns as well.

Michael was often depressed as he checked his "stats" online. With every follower that dropped, Michael would question what he had done to make it happen. Soon other friends had more followers than he did. However, he had an image to uphold, so he checked out applications that would allow him to add hundreds of friends at once, who would then follow him in return.

Michael's posts soon became nauseating. The only time he would re-tweet a post or make mention of someone else was when he or she said something flattering about him and he wanted to draw more attention to it.

Michael's church board called him in one day and told him that they thought he needed help. They told him that they loved him but that he had become so consumed with himself that he was becoming ineffective at his job. They offered him help.

Michael quit instead. He told everyone that the church didn't understand him and that they had betrayed him. He formed his own company where he became the self-proclaimed expert. In this world, Michael could be as prideful as he wanted and no one would care because he was the expert. Michael told his friends he needed to self-promote because it was how he made his living.

Michael's close friends and wife did not buy the lie. However, Michael received so many accolades from the world of "friends" he created and manipulated that he stopped listening to his real friends altogether. He stopped returning their calls. He stopped meeting with them.

Eventually, Michael drove away all the people who loved him. He has a myriad of online friends but eats his dinner by himself.

This Is Not the Place to Fight

In my mind, when we are in the midst of conflict there are levels of communication vehicles that rank as follows (starting with the most effective or least room for error). This isn't scientific necessarily, but it is based on a great deal of experience in three large churches and numerous counseling sessions with people faced with relational conflict.

1. Face-to-face

2. Phone call

3. Letter

4. E-mail

5. Social Networks and texts

Face-to-face is always best because it leaves the least room for error. In a face-to-face resolution, it is much easier to read intent because of body language, eye contact, and tone. Plus, you are less likely to go off on a tangent and spout off things in an emotional frenzy. Face-to-face gives the other person an opportunity to respond to your issues and gives you a chance to hear his or her side.

A phone call isn't bad, but it is less desirable because of the body-language element. We will always believe the nonverbal communication over the verbal. The phone allows us to "hear" what is being said but does not afford us the opportunity to match the tone against the nonverbal reinforcements such as a calm facial expression or the ability to see the veins popping out of someone's head.

A letter can be a great way to communicate, but it just seems a bit wimpy, to be honest. If you must gather your thoughts and put them all down on paper (which is usually the rationale for writing a letter), then write the letter and get together with the other party. Use the letter as a guide in your verbal communication. Make sure you tell the other party that your letter is not intended to be a list of woes but rather a way to keep you on track.

E-mail is usually horrid for conflict resolution. It can be good for setting an appointment, but that's about it. E-mail leaves so much room for misinterpretation. Make sure if you send a message to someone to set an appointment that you stay away from vague wording that might keep him or her awake at night. Be specific with your hurt so that he or she knows the issue and isn't surprised when you get together.

Wrong: "Steve, we need to get together. I have some things I need to share with you that are really bothering me."

Right: "Steve, can we get together tomorrow for lunch? I have been bothered by your recent decision regarding the youth group, and I want to make sure we talk it out."

Wrong: "Steve, hey man, we should get together and hang!"

Right: "Steve, I want to get together, but I want to be fair and let you know that I have been angry about what you said about me and I think we need to talk it through."

It is much too easy to throw up on someone and hit "send" before we have had enough time to examine our words. Most people know this. That is why they e-mail. It is fast and easy, and they get to tear someone up without having to be human; without having to listen; without having to love; without having to change.

Always use "I" messages in your conflict resolution. Do not try to build a case based on the supposed opinion of others. For example:

Wrong: "I talked to a few people after church, and they feel the same way."

Right: "I feel this way."

Wrong: "I know I am not alone in my opinion."

Right: "This is how I feel about it."

Usually, when someone says, "I talked to a few other people who feel this way," the actual scenario is, "My wife, my small group, and the other guy I complained to felt the same way after I shared my case."

By this point it is probably obvious that Social Networking leaves the most holes for proper communication in conflict resolution. It is fast, easy, and short.

In Social Networking platforms, people seldom take the time to think through what they are saying before they post it. It is usually stream-of-consciousness writing. As quickly as we think it, we easily type and hit "send." In most cases, our words are hard to take back.

This doesn't mean that we can't begin to resolve conflict in Social Networking. At times, we may find ourselves in a situation where it is wise to intercept bad communication to keep it from escalating. Consider how you might interrupt the conflict in order to put it on pause so it can be resolved in a venue where there is less room for mistakes—preferably face-to-face.

Recently, a friend of mine who is a full-time missionary posted her thoughts on short-term mission projects. Her post reflected her concerns that some of the short-term projects she was seeing in action were a hindrance to her work, as opposed to being a help.

A conversation onlooker hurled insults at her and baited a fight. Another jumped on board, and the conflict escalated. The people involved in the conflict did not know each other and came from different corners of the globe. Anybody watching the conflict unfold could have determined there would be no resolution of this conflict in any proper way. There was no way for the two at the heart of the conflict to meet face-to-face.

Many people came to the rescue of my friend, but no one had the power to squash the conflict or to resolve it. In a case like this it may be best to restrict comments or pull the post altogether. Leaving it online is neither right nor wrong, but adding to the conflict by posting your opinion may not help.

There is a series of questions you might consider if conflict situations arise in your own Social Networking platform or in others.

- Do I enjoy this conflict? If yes, I better think again about initiating or continuing my participation.

- Is this a matter of taste or preference? If so, I should question my motive for expressing my opinion or pushing my agenda.

- Is this person and the conflict he or she is stirring hurting other people with words or actions? Is this a case of defending the weak or those who have no voice? I may have a case. I may want to intercede. I may want to report the offense. I may want to just pray.

- Have I talked to this person repeatedly about the same thing? I may be right, but my further participation will probably not help.

- Have I followed the biblical principles of resolution? Is this a matter of personal offense against me or another Jesus follower?

- Is the issue at hand dragging the name of Christ through the mud? Will I further muddy the waters, or can I interrupt with a possible solution?

- Has my anger become a gateway to other sin? Is my participation in this conflict producing other results in me that are affecting my work or my family or my personal health? Have I lost control?

- In participating, do I wish ill upon another?

- Is there name-calling on my part, or am I focused on the "issue"?

- Am I willing to walk the road of reconciliation, or would I rather simply be heard?

- Are there other things that may have skewed my perspective?

- How is my own health? Spiritual? Physical? Mental?

Authentic Self, Authentic Space

People want to look their best when they go to town. They want to frequent the right shops and fit in with their wardrobe. People might feel more comfortable wearing sloppy T-shirts and sweats to town, but more times than not, because they don't want to stand out, they play by the rules.

As Jesus followers, we owe it to ourselves and to others to simply be aware of the people we meet in town. Understand, the rules are different in town. Understand, we are most likely seeing people's Sunday best—or the best thing they could come up with.

Wearing our Sunday best is not necessarily bad, but we can't pretend for long that we have no other clothes. And if we borrow someone else's clothes to go to town, someone is going to notice that they don't fit well, and we won't feel comfortable in them anyway.

Everyone wants to hang with the cool people. As Jesus followers, we have the privilege of making everyone feel welcome in the lobby. Instead of constantly drawing attention to ourselves, we have an opportunity to search out, encourage, and uplift others.

Post: Following

The Prayer Chain

The Baptist church that I grew up in had a prayer chain. Whenever someone was sick, looking for a job, had an emergency, or needed help, he or she called the church secretary. She then made a few calls to people who prayed and who called others to pray. Conversations were mostly short and sweet on the phone, but they leveraged networks. Then came the meals for the sick and the mechanics to fix the single mom's car.

When I was young, I shared with a friend that my dad was out of work and had been for some time. I came home after school that day to find my mom crying in the corner, surrounded by bags of groceries—so many that I could barely walk over to her without tripping. "What did you tell these people?" my mom asked. My friend had called his church, and they had gotten busy on the prayer chain. One thing led to another, and my family's needs were met in a very real way—to the embarrassment of my mom, who was still learning how to receive, and to the delight of my brothers and me, who realized the bags were full of goodies my mom would never buy for us.

In many ways, Social Networking has become the new prayer chain. Not that people don't still use the telephone to share prayer requests, but Social Networking has become a quick, easy way to share needs with a large group of people all at once. And it is quite effective. Whereas a telephone prayer chain would take quite some time, a quick Twitter or Facebook post takes seconds.

I brought this up to an older woman recently who told me this was the worst metaphor ever. "Why would you want to replace the old prayer chain?" she asked. She told me there was great value in the prayer chain besides the exchange of information. "The prayer chain makes us feel connected to one another in a special way when we call our friends who call other friends who call other friends. It's not just about the information; it's about the conversation."

I know where she is coming from. I encouraged her to still pick up her phone and call friends (her phone receiver, I am pretty sure, is still attached to her wall by a twenty-foot-long twisty cord). Part of this woman's argument comes from fear of change, and part of it comes from fearing that new technologies will replace something she values.

This brings up a great point. New technologies and new media seldom outright replace older ones. They do, however, teach us about what we love and value and admire about the older ones. This has always been the case.

E-mail challenged the handwritten letter or "snail mail" a few years back. And in many ways, e-mail won. It is much cheaper, faster, and more convenient. But people still love handwritten notes. Quite frankly, I usually love a thank-you card more than a quick e-mail. But that doesn't make e-mail bad. However, it does make me think about what and how I want to communicate when I am addressing others.

What I value most about the handwritten note is the time it took someone to pick it out—the care. So, if I do send an e-mail to encourage, I make sure I take the time and care that I would want someone else to take. In the same way, when I get a thank-you note that only has a signature and the sender has left the card to do the talking, I am not as impressed as I would have been if he or she had sent me a caring e-mail.

We are currently experiencing a folk music revolution. Bands like the Decemberists, Iron and Wine, Fleet Foxes, and Mumford & Sons are ruling the festival tours. This revolution is a reaction to what recent music has been missing in connection with what we value from the past. Acoustic guitars, banjos, mandolins, and violins are what all the cool people are playing. Even Robert Plant, front man of Led Zeppelin, recently teamed up with the soft-spoken beauty and golden child of bluegrass music, Alison Krauss, to make an award-winning album.

Up-and-coming Americana bands like The Steel Wheels are winning independent music awards and grabbing attention because of their fine old-school-yet-fresh musicianship and the stories their songs tell. The trend is back to grass roots; back to story; back to simple. It is a reaction against the hype of modern music with its Auto-Tuned cartooned cherubs and become-a-star-overnight pop children; a reaction against music without substantial meaning in the lyrics.

We've seen this reaction before. The 1990s brought back a loud punk-rock attitude and sounds made with standard vintage guitars (we called it "grunge") as a reaction to 1980s glam rock made by guys in tights who sold more records the faster they played and androgynous pop stars who made hits with cheesy-sounding electric keyboards.

And now, 1990s grunge god Eddie Vedder of Pearl Jam just released an album full of ballads on ukulele that you can buy at a very large national chain of coffee shops I am not allowed to mention by name (wink). Is glittery no-talent pop music going away? No. Is folk music going to rule the airwaves forever? No. We value the old. The old shapes the new. The new gives us perspective on the old. The new will become the old when another new comes along. We learn. We adapt. We change. We love it. Then we hate it. Then we love it again.

I have seen prayers answered and needs met within minutes because of Social Networking. Some of the stories have been over-the-top crazy. A pastor is given a brand-new laptop when he mentions that his has died. A full set of bedroom furniture is given to a new mom. A man gets his dream job. A sister finds her lost sibling. A daughter reunites with her dad. A family gets a reliable car. A food closet is stocked by one generous donation. An arts school gets its last-minute funding. A church budget is met, and the church keeps its good standing with the bank. A woman wins a battle with cancer, and a Bible study begins out of the people who followed her story on Facebook.

The Ultimate Social Network

Many people who hear the words *Social Networking* think of Twitter and Facebook. As I write these words, Facebook has more than six hundred million active users, and Twitter has more than two hundred million. These numbers make them the most popular Social Networking and microblogging services in the world by far. Through applications like Hootsuite, users can post things to both of these sites at the same time with the touch of a finger.

Although these are the biggest kids in the neighborhood, other sites have been around longer. MySpace beat both to the punch and maintained a fair amount of popularity after Facebook emerged, especially with musicians who took advantage of the ability to post their independent music. But as Facebook has added similar features, MySpace's user base continues to shrink.

I did a recent Google search for Social Networking sites, and the first result directed me to a Wikipedia definition of the term. At the time of this writing, there are more than two hundred Social Networking sites listed on Wikipedia that garner traffic from people who share common interests. If you are a mom, a gamer, an African American, a Christian, a homosexual, a book lover, an artist, a teenager, or you have a particular interest in the Norwegian community, there is a Social Network site for you. But Facebook still wins.

California-based Alexa Internet, Inc., ranks website traffic and continually updates a list of the most popular websites in the world. Google is consistently ranked at the top. This makes sense. Most people, when searching for anything, go to Google. Most computer users visit Google daily. What's fascinating is that Facebook ranks second in the Alexa rankings. This means that when people get on the Web for anything, they spend a significant amount of their time using Google and on their Facebook accounts.

Social Networking is a part of our lives. But it always has been.

"Wait. How can that be if these sites have been around only about a decade or less and the Internet has only been popular in homes since the mid-1990s?"

Glad you asked. Social Networking isn't just about the Web. When I was in junior college typing my papers on an electronic typewriter and using correction fluid to fix my mistakes, one of my favorite classes was sociology. One of the topics that interested me the most in the class was Social Networking. Social Networking had nothing to do with the Internet at that time. We studied people groups, like-minded student organizations, commonalities, relationships, how people respond to one another in groups, and the spread of ideas.

Even today, Wikipedia barely mentions the Internet on its page describing Social Networking. At the time of writing, its definition of Social Networking is as follows:

> A social network is a social structure made up of individuals (or organizations) called "nodes," which are tied (connected) by one or more specific types of interdependency, such as friendship, kinship, common interest, financial exchange, dislike, sexual relationships, or relationships of beliefs, knowledge, or prestige.

It is cliché to say this, but the world is changing—fast. Our language is changing fast. Definitions change fast. They change so fast that I have to include disclaimers like "at the time of writing" in this book. Social Networking is more than what happens on the Internet even if the term has adopted an online denotation.

Marketers have long understood the power of Social Networking. When I was in my twenties, it seemed like I was being asked to join Amway almost every week. As soon as someone said something to me like, "You look like the kind of guy who always has his ear to the ground for a good opportunity," I smelled soap. I went to an Amway meeting once to get a guy off my back. I remember the presenters drawing circles on a board. One circle had two lines going to two other circles. Those circles had lines going to other circles. This is Social Networking. Regardless of how you view Amway, the concept is brilliant. And it works.

Social Networking is what every home-based business and direct-sales company is built on. It's a great concept. In 2002, Warren Buffett's Berkshire Hathaway Corporation, parent company of insurance giant GEICO and paint company Benjamin Moore, acquired The Pampered Chef because it saw in it a means to harness the power of Social Networking. In two decades, The Pampered Chef has built a company, which sustains a sales force of more than sixty thousand consultants, entirely through people meeting in one another's kitchens.

Perhaps the most brilliant example of Social Networking that I can give you begins with a man from Galilee as well as a group of fishermen and a tax collector who all had one big directive in common: to follow this man Jesus and make disciples.

But that's not all they had in common.

I grew up with a mental picture of Jesus walking the shoreline and picking out guys who didn't know who the heck he was but who were so compelled by him that they just dropped everything and walked away from their nets like Stepford wives. But this isn't very realistic. I have a hard time swallowing the idea that Jesus somehow worked some charismatic magic mojo and said just the right words to make twelve hardworking men stop what they were doing and follow him around all the time, knowing nothing about him and without someone to explain their insanity to their wives.

The Bible doesn't say a lot about the disciples' lifestyle, connections, or families. We have to use common sense and acute observation of circumstances to piece things together. We don't have to make any huge theological leaps or stretch the Scriptures to see that Jesus' ministry was based on Social Networking, not random invitations to strangers.

First, there are obvious Social Networking examples like the calling of Andrew and Simon Peter. In John 1, we read that Andrew and another disciple of John the Baptist heard about Jesus through John. They asked where Jesus was staying and spent a few hours with him. We can only assume that the conversation was rich and that they asked many questions. After that time, Andrew tracked down his brother, Simon Peter, and told him, "We have found the Messiah." He brought Simon to Jesus and introduced them to each other before Simon also made a decision to follow. You tell two friends, they tell two friends, and so on and so on.

There are also the not-so-obvious-at-first-glance examples of Social Networking where we arrive at our conclusions by asking simple questions. For instance, Jesus' first miracle is in John 2. It is at a wedding. Here he turns water into wine. John tells us that Jesus' mom was at the wedding and that Jesus and his disciples were also invited. If you've ever invited people to a wedding, you know you don't invite them and then give them an invitation to invite twelve of their friends as well. People who get invited to weddings are friends and acquaintances of the bride or groom or their families or all of the above. Jesus and his disciples were all connected to one another not just through the relationship with Jesus but also through common relationships. They weren't all strangers. They had connections. They experienced life together.

When I was doing my undergraduate work at Multnomah University in Portland, Oregon, one of my most memorable classes was called "Acts-Philemon." We learned how throughout the book of Acts Social Networks had spread the gospel. Sure, we have incredible stories like that of Pentecost in Acts 2 where Peter preached and more than three thousand people responded; but after Pentecost we see the gospel spread on more of a grassroots level through everyday circumstances and ordinary people in their own sphere of influence.

My Acts-Philemon studies also taught me that the persecution of the church and the scattering of the disciples in Acts 8 played a huge role in the spread of the gospel, as it forced the church to extend outward and create new Social Networks. Of course, Roman roads allowed disciples easy access to cities around the Roman Empire. The Roman roads were literally information superhighways for early Christian ideas to spread and for new relationships to form.

Greek ideas and a shared language gave early disciples a commonality with others, which allowed them to best communicate the life to which Jesus invites us. For a great study on this, read Michael Green's *Evangelism in the Early Church*.

Colossians 3 and 4 are pregnant with words from Paul about being hospitable, starting new relationships, taking advantage of opportunities to share the gospel in conversation, living as an example in our social circles, and getting over our bad selves enough to realize our commonalities and the need to welcome everyone. Paul was a fan of Social Networking.

James Nored of the Missional Outreach Network wrote a great approachable article entitled "The Gospel Spreads through Social Networking: Lessons from Jesus and the Early Church" (www. missionaloutreachnetwork.com/profiles/blogs/the-gospel-spreads-through). Nored brings to our attention another interesting point about early Christian methodologies:

> The early Christians followed Christ, sought to be like him, and took up his call to be fishers of people seriously. Moreover, missiologist Eckhard J. Schnabel asserts that the early Christians followed Christ's life and mission even on the strategy level, for "they confessed Jesus not only as Messiah but also as Kyrios: his behavior was the model and the standard for their own behavior" (Schnabel, 1544). An examination of the early Church's outreach strategy shows that the Church followed Jesus' model of social networking.

So we don't get big heads about leading an evangelical revolution through having masses of online followers, let's remember that the role of the early disciples and apostles was not to create their own disciples but rather to point to Jesus.

In 2009, futurist and author Leonard Sweet wrote an online article entitled "Twitter Theology: 5 Ways Twitter Has Changed My Life and Helped Me Be a Better Disciple of Jesus" (www.leonardsweet .com/article_details.php?id=55). His number one observation, "Followership," is reprinted in part below. Sweet makes a wonderful connection between Jesus' strategy and methodology and those of the strategies of online Social Networking and the role of the believer:

> Twitter only knows two categories: who are you following, and who are your followers. Twitter's categorical imperative is one of followership, not leadership.

> Jesus' category is "leader." My fundamental category is "follower." Even when Jesus calls me up to the front of the line, I still lead "from behind." ... Twitter is a daily reminder that everything doesn't rise and fall on leadership but on followership—who am I following, and who is following me. ...

> Paul said "follow me as I follow Christ." In Twitter's ethic of followership, I am constantly reframing reality in ways that are more Jesus—

more grace-full, more forgiving, more loving, more humorous—and helping my "followers" to better follow Christ. I am constantly on the prowl for things that could encourage, enrich, inspire....

The Twitter question of "What are you doing?" has been replaced in my mind with "What is God doing?" and "Where do I see Jesus?" and "What am I paying attention to?"

With a new list of followers every day, and an unlimited number of potential followers, I am also reminded daily that the most important people in my life I haven't met yet.

Common language. Connections to people with connections. Venues and roads for communication and spiritual conversation. Like-mindedness. Affinity groups. Following. Finding followers. Sound familiar?

Social Networking has the incredible potential to make needs known and get needs met.

Bible Bullies, Water Guy, and the Hope Whisperer

In the summer of 2011, the twentieth annual Lollapalooza festival was held in Chicago. The sold-out music festival drew more than one hundred thousand fans. The streets surrounding Grant Park were closed off and rerouted through already busy Michigan Avenue.

Chicago looked as if hipster zombies were invading it as crowds milled about the venue in the scorching summer heat and humidity. Shoulder to shoulder, fans braved the sun to spend time with friends, celebrate life, and see their favorite bands.

Just outside the venue at the corner of Jackson Street and Michigan Avenue, a group of people stood with picket signs and megaphones. The women in the group stood huddled in a corner while one man shouted out to the crowd, "You are all headed for hell! Rock music is the devil's soundtrack! Shame on you all! The party in hell was canceled because of fire! Look at yourselves; you are disgusting!" and a few other damning and shaming words.

The crowds laughed, booed, and made hand gestures at the street preachers. One of the Bible Bullies pointed out a girl who was wearing a bikini top. He shouted at her, "If you think it's hot today, you just wait, little girl! Your father is the devil. You should be ashamed of yourself."

One of the Bible Bullies, Megaphone Man, and his sidekick pointed to a sign that read: "Women should be quiet, keepers at home, doing dishes, laundry, ironing, submissive to husbands, silent in church, caretakers of children, modestly dressed." As I walked past the Bible Bullies, one told me, "You are headed straight to hell, earrings and all. Your father is the devil. Enjoy the heat today."

On the inside of the venue was another man. He was in his midforties. He carried a five-gallon container of cool water on his back. The backpack had a pump and a sprayer hose. As the crowds waited for their favorite bands to take the stage, some people passing out from the heat, he walked through the crowds and sprayed them with cool water. People shouted out, "Hey, Water Guy! Over here! Thanks man! You're the best!" Water Guy sprayed all day with a smile.

I talked to both the Bible Bullies and Water Guy. As Megaphone Man's sidekick was verbally spanking me and telling me I needed to follow Jesus, I thought to myself, *Who would want to follow this Jesus anywhere?*

A young girl next to me came up and whispered in my ear, "Jesus isn't like this. He wasn't sent into the world to condemn the world. He wants to give people life." I just about cried. I turned to her and said, "I'm a Christian, sweetie. Thank you for those words." She got a huge smile on her face and replied, "I'm standing here listening and hurting and praying for people." "You're doing more than that," I told her. "You're taking risks by whispering hope in strangers' ears."

I don't know if Water Guy is a Christian. Quite frankly, I don't know if the Bible Bullies are either. The Hope Whisperer certainly is. One thing I know for sure, there are only two people in these scenarios that would make anyone want to follow them.

Church Culture and Leadership

For the past couple of decades the church has been fascinated with leadership. Mantras such as "Everything rises and falls on leadership" have been driving motivators for conferences, books, podcasts, and seminars.

I see more than three dozen books on leadership as I scan the bookshelves in my office. I have books on leadership habits, leadership shapes, leadership attitudes, leadership qualities, leadership mandates, leadership styles, and leadership options.

Most people in paid church positions consider themselves leaders. After all, we probably wouldn't have gotten our jobs if we weren't leaders. But the fact is, not everyone is a leader. Not everyone is called to be a leader. And Jesus certainly didn't give us the command to seek leadership.

Leadership is not a bad thing by any means. We need leaders. Someone has to take the helm. Someone needs to cast vision. Someone needs to point the way. But the reality is most of us are followers. And Jesus did indeed tell us to follow.

When was the last time you read a job description for a ministry position that said, "Must be a good follower"? Or "Must model followership characteristics"? Or "Must know how to teach good followership"?

You might think demonstrating these skills is in fact what a leader does. You're partly right. It may seem like semantics, and some of the end goals may seem the same, but it's an entirely different starting point.

The best leaders are the ones who serve people and follow examples of other leaders who do the same. The best leaders are followers of ideals, systems, and dreams. The best leaders are credible, honest, and share victories and credit for those victories. The most respected leaders never take full credit; they point to someone else with gratitude. The best leaders are the best followers.

Where are the conferences on followership? How do we become good followers? What are the habits of a good follower? Social Networking, by its very nature and structure, may be one of the best training grounds to hone skills of followership.

Follow Me as I Follow Christ

Paul's memorable words about followership are rarely quoted. His urging for people to follow him was not a statement of perfection or one where he set himself up as infallible. Rather his statement "Follow me as I follow Christ" was perfectly acceptable because of the way he phrased it. He didn't say, "I am an authority so follow me." He didn't say, "I follow Christ so listen to every word I say." He didn't say, "Follow me because I do good things." "As I follow Christ" is an important phrase for Paul.

As an early example of a follower of Jesus, Paul gave us all good instructions about living lives worthy of the name *Christian.* But he didn't set himself up as a leader. He set himself up as a follower.

Oftentimes Paul called attention to the specific things he was referring to when he talked about his example as a follower. He referred to sharing "not only God's good news with you but also our very lives" (1 Thessalonians 2:8). He made mention that his life was not "undisciplined" or idle or disorderly (2 Thessalonians 3:7). He hoped his example of diligence would prove contagious (2 Thessalonians 3:9). He was a storyteller who pointed to God and thanked God for his rescue as well as for helping him be steadfast and patient in his suffering. He told his apprentices that he saw the same characteristics in them and that they should continue to model them: "Continue with the things you have learned and found convincing" (2 Timothy 3:14).

Imagine Paul used the Internet for Social Networking purposes. Maybe he would have posted pictures of his travels, told stories of his journeys, applauded people for living well, encouraged people with words of faith and wisdom, and told stories of people who encouraged him to be a better follower. We can guess this because that is exactly what he did through the Social Network of his time.

In all Paul's examples of followership, we're encouraged to do and act likewise. His words are not just inspiration or greeting-card encouragement. They are calls to action. Followers make things happen and breed a contagious environment of other followers who do the same.

In any church environment, it is followers who get stuff done. It is followers who see dreams through to fruition. Followers feed the poor and the sick. Followers encourage others to do the same.

To encourage someone to "follow me as I follow Christ" is to encourage someone to be on the lookout for examples—to be on the prowl for stories of redemption—and to emulate them for the world to see.

I Will Follow You. Will You Follow Me?

One of my favorite things to do in the world of Social Networking is to scour the Web for people I hear are doing interesting, creative, and meaningful things for the sake of the Kingdom. When I find them in a Social Network, I click a button to "follow" them. In some networks, I have to get their permission to do so, and in others, I can simply follow. In either case, they are giving me permission to look into their lives and see what they have to say. The most inspiring people (the ones who move me to action) are the ones who tell the stories of others.

I don't look to these people as good leaders. I look to them as good followers. Good followers repeat virtuous stories. Good followers re-tweet inspiration. Good followers say, "Hey, look what this person is doing." Good followers certainly share the good things they do from time to time, but it isn't because they love the sound of their cybervoices. It's because they love the people they are associated with and want to share in the experience together as they all move forward to a common goal.

Our elder team at church is full of good people. One of the things we always ask ourselves when we include new elders is, "Are these people simply 'yes-people,' or are they willing to engage in conversation?" To be a good leader in the church, you need to know how to question, disagree well, and get your hands dirty. The leaders who know how to do these things are the true followers. They have been in the trenches. They have tried. They have succeeded and failed. But they are a lot different from the people who just sit back and say, "Sounds good to me; whatever *you* want to do." They are intimately involved with the church, the community, the people, and the mission. The only way you can do this is to follow.

If you want to be a good leader, you must first begin with the question "Am I a good follower?" We do not trust leaders who do not follow well. Whenever a politician's fidelity or military record is questioned, we automatically distrust him. It's not because we believe politicians should be infallible; it's because we want to know they have "been there" and know how to follow simple rules. No one wants to follow someone just because he or she says so. We want to follow someone who is faithful in following.

The word *disciple* shares a root with the word *discipline*. Oftentimes we think of the word *discipline* as something we hand out to others, as in "disciplining our children." But discipline is not something a leader can make happen; discipline is something a follower must be willing to do. To be true disciples, we must be willing to follow. To inspire others to be disciples, we must exhibit discipline.

The greatest Social Networking leaders are the ones who are true disciples.

Honing Our Follower Skills

In order to become effective as ministers in Social Networking, we need to know how to follow. This takes practice. When people first venture into Social Networking, they often have little clue of what this means.

"I don't want to get on Twitter," Pastor Bob told me. "I have nothing to say." Bob felt like many people do when they first venture into the Social Networking world. They resist because they have nothing to offer. In fact, Bob has a lot to offer by becoming a follower.

Bob needs to know a few things. First, there are plenty of people saying something already. Second, some people are saying things about Bob's church (and Bob). Third, some people in Bob's church are talking about their hurts, frustrations, and confusion, hoping that someone is following their story. Fourth, if Bob becomes a productive follower and active listener, he will have something to say.

Bob's hesitancy to be involved in Social Networking comes from a place within him that believes he always needs to be the leader. That reality may be true a lot of the time for Bob. When pastors are invited to dinner, they are often asked to pray. When pastors go to a barbecue, they are often asked to field questions. Many pastors feel the weight of having to be the expert 24/7. In the world of Social Networking, however, Bob has an opportunity to be "one of the people" in a way he doesn't always get to be.

Against his better judgment, Bob agreed to give Social Networking a try for six months. Thankfully, the person who dared Bob gave him some good advice to get started. That advice changed Bob's mind about what he had to offer and the validity of Social Networking as a viable ministry experience.

Bob was encouraged to go in as an "apprentice." An apprentice learns from a skilled worker in a trade by engaging in hands-on experience. This is how we learn Social Networking—by jumping in.

For the newcomer to Social Networking, it is quite common to feel out of place at first. At ground zero, we start off with no friends and no followers. This can be discouraging.

- **Let people know you're there.** Bob didn't have to say anything at the start. The fact that Bob was even in the world of Social Networking was appealing to his congregation. It communicated, "I'm available."

- **Ask questions.** Get a conversation going. Ask meaningful questions about people in your congregation and people in the community. This communicates, "I care."

- **Gather opinions.** Bob began asking opinions about the way things were going at the church. By asking the questions, Bob was not on the defense. People were kind about their opinions because he had asked. Some were not as nice, but they appreciated that he would ask in the first place. This communicates, "I'm willing to change."

- **Follow people back.** Sometimes people are afraid to follow people back if they don't know them. If someone starts tweeting distasteful things, engage her or him in conversation if it seems wise to do so. You may find that he or she is just out there to spread ill. If so, you don't have to follow any longer. However, many people will follow you because they heard something about you from a friend. Don't be afraid because you don't know them. The business of Social Networking is all about getting to know others.

- **Stand for, not against.** People love to watch a fire burn. If you are excited about Jesus, life, ministry, culture, family, art, or whatever, people will want to listen. We are attracted to people who have good news, and we want to follow them. People who always post about what is wrong in the world get boring or annoying really fast.

- **Re-tweet, repost, and "Like" what you read.** Re-tweeting is Twitter's "amen." Reposting and "liking" someone's status are the same. This spreads good news and encourages the original poster to keep posting. In the world of Social Networking, others see what you re-tweet and repost and "Like," and they search out for themselves what you draw attention to.

- **Post apt quotations.** Oftentimes, I am surprised in the middle of the day by a quotation someone posts. It encourages and inspires me. Quotations have the power to uncover a need to pay attention to what is happening around us.

- **Celebrate.** Is something great happening in the community? Tell us about it! Did God teach you a lesson? Share it. In John 4, the woman at the well went to the people of the town and blabbered with excitement about the man she had met who changed her life. Compelled by her enthusiasm, many went to hear Jesus. And many met him like she had.

- **Engage.** Watch the conversations happening around you. Jump in the middle. Your interruption is welcome. People get excited when they know others are participating. Some of the best conversations you'll ever have are the ones you don't start.

- **Answer.** One of the most compelling things about Social Networking is the ability to ask questions. Conversely, one of the most frustrating things is not to get an answer. The code of Social Networking is to answer when you're asked. People will quickly reject a person who only spouts "wisdom" without care for the little people.

- **Follow their followers.** Look at the people your friends are following. Follow them as well. Oftentimes your friends are having discussions with people you don't know well, but in the world of Social Networking, you are invited! Some of my best ongoing conversations are with people I met through someone else.

True Social Networking

Joanne was part of the small group we had in California. We haven't seen each other for years but keep in touch through Social Networking.

> "All things work together for good for those who know and love the Lord and are called according to His purpose." September 18, 2008, I got the call. "I am sorry to tell you, Mrs. Russell, but you have cancer." Those were probably the most stunning words I had ever heard in my life. And from there I faced the challenge of my lifetime.

> With that diagnosis came four major surgeries (each six months apart), chemo, the loss of my hair, forced menopause, weight gain, and an intense emotional roller coaster—not only for me but for the people I love most, my children and husband.

> I wouldn't trade the experience for anything. I often tell people that cancer was one of the best things that ever happened to me. That said, I pray I never have cancer again.

Believe it or not, social networking had a big part to play in my cancer journey and why I feel this way. After I was diagnosed, a friend created a Yahoo! Group where I could update people and share my needs. To my astonishment, more than 150 people signed up to follow me in that group and support me through my cancer journey. I was shocked at this. I had no idea so many people cared. In fact, I had no idea so many people even knew who I was.

The news spread like wildfire. Not only were people in my current community joining my group but people from the community I'd lived in three years ago were equally interested. I felt amazingly loved.

At the same time, I had discovered Facebook. Again, I was amazed at how quickly I collected friends and at all the people who wanted to connect with me.

During my treatments and surgeries, I would post on my wall. Going into my first chemo I was more scared than I had ever been in my life and I posted, "I can do all things through Christ Jesus who gives me strength. Going for my first chemo treatment today—bring it!" I must have had over twenty-seven comments on that post and an additional thirty-five likes. I felt so encouraged, loved, supported, comforted, and like I was not alone.

I quickly became addicted to Facebook. I would post and just wait and watch for a response. I couldn't believe so many people would comment and laugh on my wall. I had no idea so many people liked me. I know that sounds sad, but all my life I had been a relatively shy person. I have always been better at listening rather than sharing. Facebook showed me that people care and like what I have to say.

Cancer also gave me permission to share my faith, and people received it well. God carried me through cancer and there is no way I could have gotten through it without my faith. Through Facebook and my Yahoo! Group, I was able to share my faith and how my relationship with Jesus was getting me through.

God used my experience to share and encourage people to seek out my Savior. I was well aware of the attention and influence I had in these moments and I wasn't about to waste it. I used every opportunity to point people toward Jesus.

After my last chemo, God put it on my heart to open my home and offer a Bible study. I invited every person in my Yahoo! Group to come. Nine women came. Some unchurched, some Christian, some from various church traditions, and some who didn't have Bibles and had never even opened one came.

Together we began to study God's Word and deepen our friendships. Over the course of a year this Bible study grew to twenty-four women. At one point I had divided our groups into eight and had us meeting in small groups in three different areas of my house. My house was bursting at the seams and I was looking for a bigger place to have my Bible study.

Around that time, my church opened a venue about a mile from my house. We ended up moving my Bible study to the church and opening it up to the community and to women at my church venue. Over the course of the year, this study grew to eighty-seven women.

God is now using me to lead a ministry! By far, this has been the most rewarding and exciting experience of my life. I love every moment of my time working in this ministry.

Along the way I learned a few things. First, my confidence was dramatically boosted. I was given the privilege of knowing how much people love and care about me before I died. Second, more than ever, I learned the importance of letting your light shine for the entire world to see. Matthew 5:15 says, "Neither do people light a lamp and put it under a bowl. Instead they put it on its stand, and it gives light to everyone in the house."

Somehow, through cancer it seems, God has given me great influence and the ability to share the gospel. I have learned to use Facebook to love others, to build people up, to encourage, and to let others know I know who they are and care, and to point people toward Jesus by sharing who he is in my life. As with all things, there is a gentle and loving way to do this.

Lastly, I discovered both on Facebook and in the real world a new sense of popularity (for lack of a better word). Yes, God has created me fearfully and wonderfully. Yes, I am a fun person to know. BUT what I discovered is that people were drawn to the Jesus they saw in me. It wasn't me that people were so enamored with; it was Jesus. I am sure of it! So I continue to let my light shine for all the world to see—whether that be virtually on Facebook or in person.

Had it not been for cancer, Facebook, and my Yahoo! Group I don't think I would have ever discovered the power of having Jesus in me.

Joanne experienced the joy of her own prayer chain. I joined that conversation on Facebook, and let me tell you, we prayed for that girl.

There are bigger questions than, "Is this real community?" If we believe community is important, that God desires we pursue it, and that God wants every tribe, tongue, and nation to be a part of it, we might start with, "What am I doing to foster community?" In my church. In my world. In my family. With my neighbors. In my city.

Final Words

Social Networking is a prayer chain, a church lobby, a passing period, and the provincial life. In all these venues, people are looking for friends. They are looking for conversation. They are looking for camaraderie. They are looking for hope. They are looking for peace. They are looking for Jesus.

Imagine Jesus comes to you and says, "I have a gift for you. With this gift, you will be able to pray for people, meet needs, and see needs met. You will witness stories of redemption. You will intercede in ways you never imagined with people you don't even know that well. You will make new friends by people seeking you out. You will be blessed through this gift, and you will bless others. You will raise support and influence opinions. You will glorify my name. There are risks, but are you willing to accept this challenge?"

The time is now. The gift is real. The challenge is yours.